A History of Falkirk

LEWIS LAWSON

FALKIRK TOWN COUNCIL

1975

ISBN 0 9502250 4 5

Reprinted February 1984

Falkirk District Council
Department of Libraries and Museums
Hope Street, Falkirk

Printed by The Monument Press, Stirling

CONTENTS

ILLUSTRATIONS

ACKNOWLEDGEMENTS

I wish to place on record my indebtedness to a number of bodies and individuals who in a variety of ways have assisted in the production of this volume:

William Aitken, D.A., for providing most of the illustrative material used;

Stirling County Council for permission to use extracts and diagrams from my chapter in their publication, "The Jacobites in Stirlingshire";

The Kirk Session of Falkirk Old Parish Church for permitting me to use portions of my volume, "The Church at Falkirk";

The Falkirk Herald for permission to use sections of my articles on Old Falkirk;

The Tatler of London for permission to reproduce Lionel Edward's painting of the Battle of Falkirk;

The Royal Commission of Ancient Monuments for permission to reproduce their diagram of Arthur's O'on;

Mr Alexander Howson, Burgh Librarian of Falkirk, for supervising the arrangements for publication.

PREFACE

In all Scotland there can be few burghs of the size, importance and antiquity of Falkirk whose library shelves do not provide at least one reliable comprehensive work of local history. Falkirk is in this regard an exception. Not that the town has been without its antiquarians. Nimmo, Murray, MacLuckie, Stewart, Hunter, and that indefatiguable collector of historical snatches, Love, have all left valuable contributions to the store of local knowledge. In more recent years researches into particular topics such as the canals, the railways, the drove roads, the Church at Falkirk, the Jacobites at Falkirk, ancient monuments, the origins and development of industrial concerns, have increased the extent and accuracy of local lore. Yet there exists no single volume in which the sweep of Falkirk's story may be followed by the general reader.

It is my intention to make good this deficiency and at the same time to knit together the loose strands of the past before some become irretrievably lost. I could have chosen no more appropriate date for the publication of such a work. The year 1975 is indeed 'the end of an auld sang,' the moment when local government as we have known it will be melted in the crucible of regionalisation, bringing to a close a distinctive chapter in the burgh's history. I write this volume, however, not in the spirit of obituary. The future holds too much of promise for Falkirk to think of funeral rites.

There is of course the problem, "Which Falkirk?" The name, "Falkirk" is not exclusively reserved for the town. It is used, for instance, to give geographical location to the Roman Fort on the Antonine Wall built close on a thousand years before there was any town from which to borrow a name. For the same reason, it is associated with the two Battles of Falkirk and the Falkirk Tryst which all took place on ground which has never been or has only recently become part of Falkirk. Certain properties and industrial concerns vital to the history of the area such as Callendar House, the Canals, the Carron Iron Works, are described as being "at Falkirk" though these too have not always been encompassed by the burgh boundaries. In one instance, the name Falkirk alludes to an area far wider than the town. The medieval parish of Falkirk extended from Polmont to Castlecary and from Grangemouth to Slamannan. And even when it refers exclusively to the town, "Falkirk" means different things at different times, from the narrow belt of housing along the line of the High Street between East and West Burns to the widely scattered modern town incorporating so many once independent neighbouring communities. It is a name, moreover, applied equally to the humble huddle of dwellings with no single unit of local government which was the Falkirk of the Middle Ages, and to the Burgh of Falkirk in each of its many stages of political evolution from its feudal, laird-dominated days to its present democratic, semi-autonomous state.

In writing this volume I have not allowed myself to feel restricted by considerations of period or area. This is more the history of a name than of a town, and whenever "Falkirk" is used in a context which invites historical comment I have been ready to supply it.

January. 1975   LEWIS LAWSON

CHAPTER I

THE ROMAN FORT

To the inhabitants of that substantial cluster of dwelling houses which sprang up about the Faw Kirk in the 11th and 12th centuries, the Roman Wall must have been a dominating and enigmatic neighbour. Wherever they chose to turn southwards from their homes, there lay this impressive barrier. Well might they have marvelled at how it had come there and who had built it. Well might they have woven round it their legends and their superstitions. How many of them, farmers or herdsmen, must have cursed it for the indirect homeward path they had to tread? How many packmen or cross-country travellers must have found their curiosity superseded by exasperation as they floundered across its still deterring obstructions? How many children at their play must have stormed unscathed those defences where once the proud might of Imperial Rome stood guard?

Did they in their fancies cast themselves in the role of that Robert Graham to whom succeeding generations gave the credit of having first breached the Roman Wall? Though it is an unlikely name for a 3rd or 4th century hero, savouring rather of the Middle Ages when it was a prominent local family name, nevertheless it is as Graham's or Grim's Dyke that it became known. Grahamsdyke Street in Laurieston perpetuates the tradition and however the first conqueror of the Wall was named, he deserves some memorial for the obstacles which he had to overcome were formidable.

First was a high mound, flattened at the summit to deny the intruder cover, fashioned from earth cast out of a deep V-shaped ditch, forty feet wide and twelve to fourteen feet deep into which they must slither and out of which they must climb before reaching a stretch of open ground some twenty feet from the base of the wall. The wall itself stood fully ten feet high, a turf wall on a stone base fourteen feet wide narrowing to six feet at its top. To protect patrols, a palisade of wood raised the effective height on the North side to between fifteen and twenty feet.

The wall was well defended by auxiliary troops brought from as far afield as France, Spain, the Lower Rhine, Thrace and Syria. Every two miles there was a fort. Between forts small watch towers or

11

Fosse in Callendar Park

fortlets may have been built to give shelter to the patrols who ceaselessly searched across the Carseland of Forth for signs of an enemy they had learned to respect. If danger threatened, smoke signals by day and fire by night would summon support which would pour along the military road running the length of the wall some fifty yards to the south.

It is a testimony to the men who built this impressive barrier, all citizens of Rome of the 2nd, 6th and 20th Legions, that after close on 2000 years the results of their labours have not been wholly erased, and this, despite the enormous urban, industrial and communications revolution of the last century. In the grounds of Callendar Park, the ditch and flat ground on which the wall stood may still be seen. The line westward from this point was across the East Burn towards the Pleasance where the wall plunged down into the West Burn and climbed up Arnothill, crossed Maggie Wood's Loan, and thence passed through the grounds of Bantaskine and on to close by Lock Sixteen. Thereafter comes another fine section of the wall, perhaps the finest part of the ditch anywhere to be seen. It ends at Watling Lodge where until 1894 there was a small fortlet, no doubt built to safeguard the point where the chief Roman road from the south cut through the Wall on its way north, as far as is known the only place in the whole length where a Roman route passed through the wall.

The reason for this singular feature seems to lie in the high strategic value of Camelon where a fort defended the crossing of the River Carron. Beside this fort great supply depots were maintained for the supply of armies stationed further north. Camelon seems to have been at the centre of considerable military activity throughout the Roman period. At least two large camps were built at different times and several temporary marching camps were occupied.

One intriguing feature of the Antonine Wall is the fort at Falkirk. Forts on the wall are distinguished by their lack of uniformity in size and constructional material. Some are as large as Mumrills at Laurieston, 6½ acres. Others are small like Roughcastle which was only an acre in extent. But large or small they are evenly spaced, 2000 yards between each. So there must clearly have been a fort somewhere within the boundaries of what is modern Falkirk. The site most favoured is at the Pleasance-Arnothill area where the Wall crossed the West Burn. Was it large or small? Did it have the usual buildings —the headquarters block, officers' quarters, granaries, workshops, stores, barracks, baths? More intriguing still, did it have an annexe? The purpose of an annexe was initially to house the drivers and craftsmen who worked for the Romans. Later, however, trading posts and dwelling houses sprang up and places of entertainment for the off-duty soldiers were opened. Native families moved into these annexes and were joined by the wives and children of Roman soldiers. If such a community did emerge at Falkirk, then it can be confidently stated that this was the first large civilian settlement ever established in the area.

The interest of the Romans in this particular region of North Britain was spread over three hundred years. The accident of geography which provided a potential defence line between Forth and Clyde only thirty-seven miles wide was not lost to the Roman warlords. As early as 78-84 AD, Julius Agricola had sought to safeguard the newly won province of Southern Britain by a line of forts thrown across this strategic isthmus. The lesson of this type of defence was soon learned. No matter how well patrolled, Agricola's forts, at least one of which stood at Falkirk, were not sufficient to prevent serious inroads being made by a determined enemy thrusting from the safety of his native hills across the marshes and interlacing streams of the Forth valley.

When next the Romans contemplated a defence line between Forth and Clyde, the Antonine Wall was the result. Just after 139, when Lollius Urbicus was Governor, a resolute effort was made to destroy and contain the threat from the North. Actual events are shrouded, but in 142 a great victory was won over the Northern tribes, a success commemorated by coins struck at that time. It is tempting to place the site of this decisive battle close to present-day Falkirk. Inside what were the Stenhouse policies between Carron Ironworks and Stenhousemuir, there stood until 1743 a Roman temple called by the locals, "Arthur's O'on," which may well have been a victory monument

erected on the battlefield. It resembled a beehive, was 22 feet high and almost 20 feet in diameter at its base. Unfortunately this priceless link with ancient times survived the barbarism of the Dark and Middle Ages only to be cast down by a modern vandal, the Laird of Stenhouse, for no better purpose than to obtain cheap stone with which to repair a mill dam.

The victory of 142 made the building of the Wall of the Emperor Antoninus Pius possible. Its effective life span was, however, relatively short. By 196 the Roman legions and auxiliaries were withdrawn and the wall was forsaken, and though the Emperor Severus did mount a military expedition to the Forth-Clyde line early in the 3rd century, by 210 he had decided that henceforth the Romans would place their reliance rather upon the Hadrian Wall between Tyne and Solway.

The departure of the legions did not mean that Roman influence was completely removed. Roman roads continued to be used until the 18th century. Valuable treasure trove from the sites of forts was discovered over the centuries. The Wall, too, served as a boundary, a recognisable landmark, a convenient trysting place for men of peace and men of less reputable intent. It was a place of wonder, of mystery, of superstitious dread, of intriguing conjecture, not least the thought that where Falkirk now stands was once the most northerly frontier of an Empire stretching southward as far as the sands of Sahara, and Eastward along the Rhine and the Danube to those cradles of ancient civilisation, Egypt and Persia.

CHAPTER II

THE FAW KIRK

With the exception of the Roman Wall, Falkirk's longest link with antiquity is that sacred acre on which Falkirk Old Parish Church now stands. It is true that there is no evidence stronger than tradition for placing the foundation of the Christian Church at Falkirk in the late 6th—early 7th centuries when a St. Modan carried Celtic Christianity across Central Scotland from Iona. Whether he used a cell at Falkirk as a base for his missionary activities will never be substantiated. Nevertheless, on this mound reputedly hallowed by the saint, the people of the area, speaking Gaelic or some kindred Celtic tongue, had by the 11th century built a church using stones sufficiently varied in colour to earn church and district the name "Eglais Bhreac" or spotted kirk.

It is thus called in 1080 when Symon of Durham records that a Norman pursuit of Northumbrian rebels against William the Conqueror ended at Egglesbreth, the anglicised form of Eglais Bhreac. In the 12th century, the Chronicles of Holyrood Abbey refer on several occasions to the "Ablands" of Falkirk. "Ablands" is a term invariably used in documents of the Roman Catholic Church after 1100 to indicate lands owned at one time by Celtic monasteries, so there is further evidence of a Celtic foundation at Falkirk in the 11th century or earlier.

By the 12th century, the Roman Catholic Church had supplanted the Celtic form of religion, and chroniclers were using a Latin version of "Eglais Bhreac." This form appears in the Charter of Holyrood Abbey referring to "Ecclesia de Egliasbreac qui *Varia Capella* dicitur." By the 13th century there is yet another variation. With the spread of the English tongue, "Varia" becomes "Faw," and "Capella" becomes "Kirk," so that quite apart from its religious and social service, the Christian Church provided the town with the name by which it was hereafter to be known.

There is no exact date for the first Roman Catholic congregation at Falkirk. It is certain, however, that in the 12th century Falkirk was part of the Roman Catholic Church organisation. Bishoprics were being set up and within each bishopric smaller units, deaneries and parishes, were emerging. Falkirk was a parish in the Deanery of Linlithgow which was one of the eight deaneries of the Bishopric of St. Andrews. The Deanery of Linlithgow had 35 churches, the most richly endowed of which were St. Cuthbert's, Edinburgh, cessed at 160 merks, Falkirk cessed at 120 merks and Linlithgow cessed at 110 merks. The average yield from all 35 churches was 41 merks so that the importance of Falkirk is evident. It would be misleading however to imagine that Falkirk was in any way wealthy. These were days of abject poverty and the parish was distinguished for its extent rather than for its riches. To the south, its boundary ran close to Slamannan. To the West the parish stretched to Castlecary and embraced Bonnybridge and Denny. To the North it shared a common boundary with Larbert, Airth and Bothkennar. To the East it included Grangemouth, Polmont and Muiravonside.

Just when the new system of bishopric and parish was emerging, its course was changed by the practice of monarchs, churchmen and nobles making lavish grants of land and properties to monasteries, nunneries and priories. Thus in 1166 Richard, Bishop of St. Andrews, bestowed the Church at Falkirk upon the Augustinian Canons of Holyrood Abbey, keeping a nominal interest in Falkirk by exacting an annual payment of a stone of wax. Thus the Church at Falkirk and a fair portion of the land in and around the town passed to the black-cassocked, white-surpliced Augustinians. These churchmen were not cloistered but were free to move about the parish churches under their patronage. No doubt in the early days they brought certain benefits. They did something to improve agriculture. They built the Ladysmill using the waters of the East Burn to turn its wheel. They brought what little education existed in a dark age and promoted choral singing in worship. However the balance was weighted on the debit side. The tithes, endowments and offerings all went to the Abbey, a mere pittance returning to pay the priest. Several days' unpaid service in the fields or cutting peats or gathering firewood or carrying loads were demanded from bondsmen. And as the centuries passed and monastic standards fell disastrously, Falkirk and similarly assigned parishes felt even more acutely the yoke of an absentee, feudal landlord more concerned with the revenues to be exacted than the souls to be saved and the service to be supplied.

Nothing now remains of the Church which served Falkirk in those grim, medieval times. About 1450 the sound of masons' chisels and carpenters' hammers proclaimed the building of a new church on the site of the first Faw Kirk. It was a church typical of its age, cruciform in shape with a high altar to the east and the crossing situated where

The Faw Kirk 1450-1811

now is found the vestibule of the modern church. Above the crossing was built a tower resting on four piers set in the angles of transept and nave. The lower part of the tower was of stone, but timber and slates were used in the construction of the upper section. Two of the piers of the south crossing may be seen today embedded in the modern walls at the entrance to choir and session rooms. They bear masons' marks and are 15th century in design.

But the new church was not symbolic of a new age. Only the skyline of Falkirk was changed. Well might the citizen of that mean huddle of dwellings that were medieval Falkirk bitterly contemplate the apparent changelessness of the lot of the lowly-born. Today, a new church in which to worship, but tomorrow the same leech-like presence of the Augustinian Canons, the same feudal injustices, the same eternal battle against hunger, disease and the harsh relentless climate.

CHAPTER III

THE FIRST BATTLE OF FALKIRK

"On the day of the Magdalen after midsummer the people of Scotland each with a spear in fist are come to Falkirk in a morning." So did one of the chroniclers of the time, Pierre de Langtoft, set the scene for what was to be known as the First Battle of Falkirk. For three years William Wallace had hurled defiance at English claims to govern Scotland. One English army had been destroyed at Stirling Bridge, Northumberland had been invaded and the very gates of Newcastle assaulted. Tales of Scottish atrocities south of the Border brought calls for vengeance. Edward I, free at last from immediate troubles in his French possessions, was not slow to respond. Scotland must be taught a lesson that rebellion does not pay, and he was willing to be the teacher. With the biggest single army ever mustered by an English monarch, he set out for Scotland. The main force marched overland encamping at Kirkliston early in July, 1298. The remainder came by sea, disembarking at Blackness on 20th July.

There are considerable difficulties in attempting to measure the number of troops involved. According to the Exchequer Rolls 14,800 men were in Edward's pay in Scotland on 20th July, but many soldiers fought at the expense of their feudal overlords and would not be listed. The Falkirk Roll of Arms drawn up by Henry Percy naming the most important men in the army details 110 nobles commanding retinues. It would not therefore be unreasonable to put the English numbers at Falkirk at some 25,000 infantry and several thousand cavalry.

Scottish numbers cannot be reckoned accurately. There are no exchequer or muster rolls as in England. The records of the time are notoriously biased. English chroniclers exaggerate Scottish numbers in order to flatter the victors. Walter of Guisborough actually estimates the Scottish force at well over 300,000, more men than lived in the country at that time. Rishanger puts the Scottish figures at 100,000. Scottish chroniclers on the other hand tend to underestimate the size of the Scottish army. From descriptions of the battle and of their disposition at its outset, it would appear that the Scots were not fewer in numbers than their foes, perhaps 30,000.

The Scottish force was, however, far from united. In those feudal days when high birth brought precedence over men of more lowly station, Wallace found his position as Guardian of Scotland most delicate. He was constantly beset with the jealousy and antagonism of the nobles in his company. Several chroniclers describe council disputes, in one of which Wallace actually offered to resign his charge in favour of any noble acceptable to the others. In another report, however, Wallace stoutly refuses to abdicate except to his rightful king then a prisoner in England. Comyn, whose claim to the Scottish throne was superior to any, refused to continue under Wallace's command, and Fordun says marched his force away from the battle-field of Falkirk as far as Cumbernauld taking no part in the engagement. It must be borne in mind that the chronicles were all written after the accession of Robert Bruce, the great adversary of the Comyn family, when there was political profit to be gained in discrediting the Comyns. The departure of Comyn might however explain the discrepancies in the source material, some chroniclers writing of four, and others of three, Scottish divisions in the field.

Yet another rebel against Wallace's authority was Stewart of Bonkhill, Principal of Bute and brother of the Lord High Steward of Scotland.

"The gud Stewart of But com to the land
With him he ledys weill ma than twelf thousand."

Blind Harry, Henry the Minstrel, author of the Scots historical poem, "The Actis and Deidis of the Illustere and Vailzeand Campioun Schir William Wallace, Knicht of Ellerslie" reports that Stewart demanded the right to lead the Scots:

"The Steward said he would the vanguard have;
Wallace answered and said "So God me save
That shall ye not so long as I may reign
Nor no man else until I see my right king."

Though Stewart remained to fight most valiantly on the day, there may be substance in the suggestion that he withdrew his force outwith Wallace's command. Some sources certainly speak of the Men of Bute fighting apart, one indeed going so far as to condemn Wallace for leaving Stewart to face the English attack alone. This story is not corroborated by Fordun or Hearn or any of the English chroniclers, none of whom leaves an impression that only one Scottish unit was engaged. Blind Harry, however, sums up the discord thus:

"Alas gret harm fell Scotland through that strife."

Wallace could not but be alarmed at these pre-battle wrangles and at the open hostility shown him by the lords of Scotland. These men were his professional soldiers, trained from boyhood in war, and

19

providing him with his only cavalry on which he must place great reliance in view of the formidable body of horsemen which opposed him. He was well aware that quite apart from their resentment at being led by a commoner they were torn in their loyalty. Many were Anglo-Norman by extraction and felt no strong national fervour. Many indeed were landowners in England as well as in Scotland and had paid homage to Edward for their southern estates. All recognised that they were hazarding much in defying the great English warrior king.

It was an uneasy Wallace then who on 22nd July watched the approach of the English host from Linlithgow where they had spent the night. The English monk Hemingford who was an eyewitness of the engagement writes that the Scottish force came into view drawn up on high ground above the town of Falkirk. William of Malmesbury also speaks of high ground near the town, and there seems no good reason to doubt that the Scots occupied the site traditionally accepted, a location at Wallacestone. Local historians who have sought to site the battle to the north of Falkirk in the Victoria Park or Mungal areas, or even in Grangemouth, ignore the nature of the terrain in those days. It was no accident that the main road from Linlithgow to Stirling followed the 100 foot contour, placing it above the low lying bog land of the Carse. Certainly in the latter phases of the battle the pursuit carried into these areas but initially the ground chosen by Wallace was suited to give firm footing for his spearmen drawn up into close-packed schiltroms of some 10,000 men. Several chroniclers write of long poles being set into the ground angled to meet oncoming horsemen. Between the schiltroms stood groups of archers, while in the rear was placed the cavalry on which disposition Wallace relied to resist the English superiority in mounted men. It is interesting that the chief concern of the Scots was English horsemen not their archers, a clear indication that the longbowman was not yet rated as the decisive force in war which he became in the following centuries. Thomas Walsingham in the St. Albans Chronicle has Wallace casting a taunt at the English King from behind his prepared position:
"Now I have brought you to the ryng, hoppe zif ye kanne."

Edward I, nursing ribs and a leg injured in a fall from his horse on the previous day, had placed the banner with its three leopards over his headquarters by Laurieston. He began directing footmen and cavalry into position. It was not yet noon. The hour of retribution or of liberation had come. He signalled the attack.

It was the cavalry which made the first onslaught. As the horsemen drove up the hill, the Scottish spears lowered, their butts firmly grounded, their points obliquely slanted towards the onrushing English tide. It was that awesome moment before collision . . . the

20

drumming of hoofbeats, cheer and counter-cheer, battlecry on battlecry, last nervous adjustments to foot and spear, to shield and lance. And then the clash . . . and instant confusion. Horsemen tumbled from rearing mounts shying away from that grim forest of Scottish spears. Others fell headlong into the Scottish ranks as the very intensity of their approach caused the cruel steel to burst through their horses' body armour. Those unseated were bowled over by the second wave of cavalry pressing immediately behind. On all sides there were the cries of wounded men and the agonised whinneying of horses. English knights who managed to find gaps in the Scottish spear wall were dragged from saddles and butchered by foes who gave no quarter. And as spearman stolidly stepped forward to fill the breach left by a fallen comrade, the schiltrom remained intact and defiant to third and fourth waves of cavalry toiling up the hillside. And suddenly it was over. The English force was in retreat. The schiltrom had held fast. A full-throated Scottish roar of triumph resounded after the fleeing foe. They rejoiced too soon.

Edward grimly ordered a second cavalry assault which fared no better. It was then the turn of the footman, and from that moment the whole complexion of the engagement changed. The English bowmen had little difficulty in finding targets for the twenty-four arrows in their quivers amid the close-packed Scottish ranks. Wide gaps appeared in the schiltroms. Then came a respite as the English archers ran out of arrows. Nothing daunted they began gathering stones which they hurled at the Scottish footmen. At this point with the fate of the battle still in the balance, the English cavalry returned. Wallace swung round to wave forward his own horsemen held in reserve for just this moment. The hillside was empty. To a man they had deserted and later on that day would beg forgiveness from their English overlord.

Without opposition the English knights quickly exploited the weaknesses in the schiltroms. As they drove deep wedges into the heart of the Scottish formations the Scots broke and thereafter the battle spilled in all directions, English and Welsh troops eagerly following up for the kill. The conduct of the Welsh contingent is remarked upon by several chroniclers. Drunk with wine taken on empty stomachs, they refused to fight and were attacked and some eighty slain by English forces. They took no part in the assault but did join in the rout.

The remainder of the battle is the story of a number of separate engagements. One English knight, Brian de Jay, headmaster of the Temple, pursued his enemy to a river crossing where he was unseated as his horse stuck in mud. He died still resisting and it may well be

Bute Memorial

that he gave his name to that place, Briansford or Bainsford. Elsewhere Stewart was struck down after a valiant stand against impossible odds. As he lay mortally wounded, his Men of Bute refused to forsake him, ringed their fallen chief, being themselves cut down until not a man survived. The brave story of the Men of Bute inspired the erection of the Celtic Cross at the West end of the Parish churchyard. Its legend reads:

"In memory of the Men of Bute who under Sir John Stuart on 22nd July, 1298 in the Battle near the Fawe Kirk fought bravely and fell gloriously this Cross is reverently raised by John Stuart, Marquess of Bute AD 1877."

Stewart was laid in the churchyard, and the present gravestone may well be the original for it is typical of the 13th century with its coffin shape and bevelled edges. It lies on the right of the path entering from

22

Stewart of Bonkhill Grave Stone

Manse Place. In the Old Statistical Account reference is made to this stone having no inscription and the present lettering is 19th century:
    "Here lies a Scottish hero, Sir John Stewart who was killed at the Battle of Falkirk 22nd July, 1298."

The most notable casualty in the Battle was undoubtedly Sir John de Graeme, the young man who had fought alongside Wallace from the time of Stirling Bridge. The death of Wallace's right hand man is one of the most noteworthy passages in the eleven books which make up Blind Harry's chronicle. It tells how de Graeme fought and killed an English knight. So intent was he on the encounter that he failed to observe another enemy creeping up behind him. Graeme's corselet was not properly jointed at the waist and the newcomer struck him through the gap. To make doubly sure that he did not escape, his horse was slain. According to Blind Harry, Wallace sought out the body and carried it to the churchyard at Falkirk for burial. In actual fact he must have been too pre-occupied in making his escape to the Torwood. Nevertheless there is a touching passage which has affected readers down through the ages. Wallace dismounting and taking de Graeme in his arms, kissed him and called him his best Brother,
    "My faithful friend when I was hardest stead
    My hope, my health thou wast in most honour
    My faith, my help my strenthiest in stoure . . ."

23

There follows a recital of knightly virtues:

"In thee was wit, freedom and hardiness
In thee was truth, manhood and nobleness
In thee was rule, in thee was governing,
In thee virtue without varying
In thee was loyalty, in thee was largesse
In thee gentility, in thee was steadfastness . . .
They carried him with worship and dolour
Into Fawkyrk graith'd him in sepulture."

It is most likely that de Graeme's first gravestone was similar to that which covered Sir John Stewart. However when Blind Harry's poem was published in 1570 it may have occasioned the erection of the first slab resting on four pillars which certainly was in position in 1697.

De Graeme Tomb

Around its edges runs the epitaph:

"Heir lyes Sir John the Grame baith wight and wise
Ane of the chiefs wha rescewet Scotland thris;
Ane better knight not to the world was lent
Nor was gude Grame of truth and hardiment."

At the head of the stone may be seen a panel shaped like a rose bearing the motto, "Vivit Post Funera Virtus." In the centre of the

24

slab is the device of a shield with the heron as its crest and two further herons as supporters. The motto on the shield is "Ne oublis." At the foot of the slab is a raised panel with a Latin inscription. Translated it reads, "Potent in mind and hand and the faithful Achates of Wallace, Graeme is buried here slain in war by the English 22nd July, 1298."

A modern Scots Version of "The Wallace" in 1722 may have inspired the addition of the second slab to the tomb, and yet another slab, placed six inches above the 1723 slab was provided by William Graham of Airth in 1773. Finally in 1860 a public subscription led to the erection of "that elegant and appropriate railing with Gothic cupola which now encloses the tomb of the gallant Graeme." Also in 1860 a replica of the sword reputedly used by de Graeme was cast at Falkirk Iron Works from the original in the possession of the Auchterarder No. 46 St. John's Lodge of Freemasons. Unfortunately vandals have left only the central position of the casting which renders this curiously hybrid memorial untidily incomplete.

How many men died in this encounter will never be known. On the English side there is some indication in that the number of men in the King's pay on 27th July was 2,200 fewer than on 20th July. Scottish casualties must certainly have been very much higher though not of the astronomical proportions claimed by English chroniclers.

So the dead pits were dug and mothers and widows mourned, and Edward could boast of victory and take satisfaction in the fact that Wallace was unlikely again to be a powerful force in the land. Yet, hard-headed man of the world that he undoubtedly was, did he really believe that he had finally hammered the Scots? Testimony to the futility of war came only sixteen years later when across the very fields where the English had raised their triumphant huzzas, streamed the sorry remnant of another English force fleeing from Bannockburn where Robert Bruce, one of the nobles who treacherously defected from Wallace's command at the crucial moments of the fight at Wallacestone, effectively forged with blood and iron the Scottish nation which Edward had hoped to bury on St. Magdalen's Day in the charnel pits at Falkirk.

CHAPTER IV

CALLENDAR AND FALKIRK

As long as there has been a Falkirk it has had a neighbour, Callendar. Those who seek a derivation of the name in Roman times when the Calones were wood-gatherers for the Roman forces do not satisfactorily explain how the term became attached to this particular estate. It is certainly too far-fetched that any of the Calones, the lowliest menials in the Roman camps and notoriously simple-minded, could ever have established a personal estate of Callendar during the days of the Roman occupation. It would seem that this conjecture is an over-ingenious attempt to relate the billets in the Callendar crest now incorporated in the Falkirk Coat of Arms with remote antiquity.

In the 13th century, Malcolm of Kalynter first enters recorded history as feudal lord of Callendar, a Charter of King Alexander II issued on 26th August, 1239 confirming to "Malcolm, son of Duncan . . . the lands of Calynter he had from the King." It is not surprising that billets of wood should have featured in the family crest because the estates were well wooded, and the forests of Callendar appear in a number of medieval documents as a region wherein tenants had rights of gathering firewood. It has been suggested, alternatively, but without corroboration that the billets represent manuscript scrolls indicating that the lairds had a clerical or legal function.

Malcolm and his descendants built at Callendar a fortified dwelling but no specific information exists as to its nature. In that it was a 13th century construction it would almost certainly have been a manor house or stone tower. Malcolm's son may be the "Alwinus de Kallenter, miles de counte de Strivelyn" (knight of the county of Stirling) noted in the writs of the 1250s and in a lawsuit remitted to Pope Innocent IV who was asked to give judgement on Alwin's legal title to the estates, he being reputedly a bastard son.

Alwin's successor was Patrick of Kallenter who sided with Edward I in 1299. Either he or a successor by the same name joined Edward Balliol against David II in 1345 and in consequence had his estates confiscated.

26

The new proprietor was Sir William Livingstone who had been captured along with the King at the Battle of Durham in 1346, an event which was not wholly a misfortune for Sir William because he obtained a Charter under the Great Seal naming him Lord of the lands of Calynter. In order to consolidate his title to his newly acquired estates he married Christiane de Calynter, daugher of the ousted Patrick.

So began a long association of the Livingstone family with the affairs of Falkirk for amid their wide territories part of the town fell under their feudal jurisdiction.

The new proprietors almost immediately began the construction of a tower house at Callendar, the remains of which embedded in the north-west corner of the present building are the oldest stonework now existing. The most powerful and influential of the Livingstones was the third laird, Sir Alexander, who became prominent after the murder of James I at Perth in 1436. Gaining possession of the person of the young King, James II, he was able to exert great pressure on the

The Livingstone Effigies

27

course of national events. Lindsay of Pitscottie and Buchanan in their histories name him Regent, but the evidence of the Exchequer Rolls shows that the Earl of Douglas had this nominal title throughout the period. Whatever his title, however, Livingstone was for a time the virtual ruler of Scotland until the King was old enough to take personal charge. Sir Alexander died in 1451 and may have been buried in the South Aisle of the new Faw Kirk which was built in the 1450s. The pair of effigies in the eastern passage of the Parish Church may represent Sir Alexander and his wife. Another possibility is that they represent Sir Alexander's son, James, First Lord Livingstone of Callendar, Great Chamberlain of Scotland who died in 1467. The style of the effigies would fit the mid-15th century period. Though the head of the male figure is almost worn away, his breastplate reveals traces of a coat of arms. There is a sword at his side. His wife's dress has a tight fitting bodice from which the skirt hangs in folds, and a mantle is draped from the shoulders to the feet.

One of the Livingstone family, Sir Henry of Livingstone was Preceptor of the Order of Knights Hospitallers in 1463 and had his chapel in the South Transept of the Kirk at Falkirk. For this reason the Livingstones became associated with this chapel in which they buried their dead. After 1811 when the present church was built the effigies were subjected to much weathering. When in 1892 the South Porch and Hall were added to the church, the effigies again were brought under cover. In 1970, however, in the course of extensive rebuilding operations, they were moved into the corridor of the church to permit redevelopment of the porch to proceed.

During the 15th and 16th centuries several extensions were made to the Towerhouse at Callendar. An East Wing was constructed, making the house one of the most impressive in the county. Mary, Queen of Scots, spent some of her earliest days at Callendar House where the fifth Lord Livingstone was her guardian. It was while she was yet an infant that the Scottish leaders meeting at Callendar House on 4th September, 1543, tore up the Treaty of Greenwich by which Mary was espoused to marry Prince Edward, son of Henry VIII of England. Henry, furious at the failure of his plans to unite England and Scotland by marriage, unleashed the Hertford Raids, the so-called Rough Wooing, devastating much of the Border country and burning the port of Leith in an effort to persuade the Scots to renew the alliance. After the further invasion of 1547 when the Regent Somerset continued the policy of terrorising the Scots, Mary was sent to France accompanied by Lord Livingstone and the four Maries, one of whom was Mary Livingstone. He never again saw Scotland for he died in France. An old grave slab dug out of the floor of the South Porch in 1970 bears the legend:

."ALE(xander) ADOLESCENTIAM PROVECTAM AE TATEMINiVLA REGUM GALLIAE." The reference to "Alexander," to "protector in youth" and to "the kingdom of France" may indicate that the stone is a memorial to Alexander. A further proof may be that his second wife was Agnes Douglas and the Douglas device is to be seen on the slab alongside that of Livingstone. This slab is now fixed to the wall in one of the corridors of the Parish Church.

Alexander was succeeded by his son, William who proved himself just as devoted to Queen Mary's cause. After her return to Scotland in 1561, Mary was a frequent visitor at Callendar House, actually attending a baptismal service in the Protestant form of one of Lord Livingstone's children. The Queen's bedroom during these visits was in the north-west portion of the house and is clearly marked over the door for present-day visitors. She slept there in 1567 on her way to Glasgow to meet Darnley. A few days later, she and Darnley returned by way of Callendar House en route for Edinburgh and that series of tragic events which saw Darnley murdered, the Queen married to Bothwell, her defeat at Carberry Hill and her imprisonment at Loch Leven Castle. Livingstone stayed a Queen's man throughout being implicated in escape bids and when she finally did succeed, joining her with men from Falkirk at the Battle of Langside where her cause was lost. He and his wife accompanied her into exile in England and during her long captivity he was constantly engaged in trying to restore her fortunes. When Elizabeth limited the number of the Queen's attendants, Lady Livingstone was allowed to return to Callendar House by the Regent Morton on condition that she took no part in any conspiracy. Her letters to the Queen's Lords were however discovered and she was imprisoned in Dalkeith Castle until Sir Alexander Bruce of Airth agreed to act surety for her good conduct. After Mary's execution at Fotheringay in 1587, Lord William returned to Callendar House where he died in 1592. The second set of effigies in the Parish Church may represent Lord William and his wife, Agnes Fleming, a tangible link with one of the most dramatic and stirring periods of Scottish history.

The career of the Seventh Lord Livingstone, Alexander, son of Lord William, brought significant advancement not only to the fortunes of the Livingstone family but also to the development of Falkirk. At the time of the Gowrie Conspiracy in 1600, Alexander with men from Falkirk marched against the rebels in time to save the king. As a token of royal trust, James VI placed his daughter, Elizabeth, under his protection so that part of her childhood was spent at Callendar House. Elizabeth was ultimately to marry Frederick of the Rhine

Palatinate and provide the Hanoverians with the link through which they could lay claim to the British throne.

Further evidence of royal regard came in 1600 when Falkirk was created a Burgh of Barony with Livingstone as its Baron Bailie. Six years later he was further honoured being created First Earl of Linlithgow.

By a happy coincidence almost immediately after the formation of the Burgh of Barony there occurred a change of ownership of that part of Falkirk not under the jurisdiction of the lairds of Callendar. As has been seen, the Abbey of Holyrood was feudal overlord of lands on the north and east side of the town. Besides his control over the Parish Kirk the Abbot could claim superiority over Kirk Wynd, the Back Row (modern Manor Street), the Randygate (modern Kerse Lane), Ladysmill and adjoining lands. In 1393 these holdings were joined into the Barony of Abbot's Carse (Kerse). In the century which preceded the Reformation the enormous wealth and privileges of the monasteries attracted unscrupulous men who contrived to gain titular office in the church in order to lay hands on its rich revenues.

The monarch himself was not averse to joining in this scramble. James V secured the Abbey of Holyrood and with it the Barony of Abbot's Carse and the tithes of Falkirk Parish Church on behalf of one of his illegitimate sons, then an infant. After the Reformation in 1560 the pretext of elevating the collector of revenues to office in the church was abandoned, the layman given the right being said to hold the benefice "in commendam," i.e., in trust. In 1584 the commendator of Abbot's Carse was Sir John Bellenden whose son, Lewis, married Margaret, daughter of Lord William Livingstone. In 1587 Lewis Bellenden, Baron Broughton, received "the land of Falkirk with cottages, part and pendicles of the same and the right of patronage of the kirk at Falkirk with its whole tithe sheafs." On his death these rights and properties passed to his son, Sir James Bellenden who in 1606 conveyed them to his uncle Alexander, Seventh Lord Livingstone. Thus Alexander was able to extend his baronial jurisdiction over the whole of Falkirk which for the first time in its five hundred years of civic existence could have at least the semblance of a unified corporate life.

Alexander was the last of the Livingstones to escape relatively unscathed the upheaval and insecurity wrought by the contest between the Scottish Kirk and the Crown. He was of course not unaware of the latent danger of such strife. From the 1560s the new Protestant churches had been governed by Kirk Sessions made up of minister and elders. Falkirk had its first Protestant minister, Alexander Forrester inducted in 1574. Indeed Alexander was himself a member of the Kirk Session his name appearing first in the list of elders in the earliest minute of Kirk Session inscribed on 21st August, 1617. It was not, however, at this level of church organisation that the real controversy arose. Nor was it at the higher levels of the church courts. By 1562 Synods, provincial courts, and the General Assembly, the national court were well established. It was over the question of what type of organisation to place between these higher courts and the Kirk Sessions that the great dispute arose which was to tug parish churches such as Falkirk and indeed the whole nation this way and that for over a century.

The royal preference was to revive the office of Bishop which gave the King a firm control over the Kirk. Progressive elements however denounced bishops as relics of the Old Faith and declared all ministers equal and bishops unlawful. They recommended instead an area court made up of laymen and ministers to which the name Presbytery was given. In this new arrangement, the Kirk at Falkirk was to be part of the Presbytery of Stirling until 1608, though by 1614, it had been reallocated to the Presbytery of Linlithgow.

If the new generation of churchmen had been content to let matters rest there the story of the Church at Falkirk and in Scotland would have been different. However they went on to declare that the authority of the General Assembly was distinct from that of the state. There were two kingdoms "One of Christ Jesus the King and His Kingdom the Kirk, whose subject James the Sixth is . . ." Here were claims that threatened the whole foundation of monarchy. Behind the King stood the great landowners who saw that if the Kirk made good its claim, it would not be long before it was demanding the restoration of those lands and properties seized at the time of the Reformation. Townsmen were also alarmed for if the Crown could no longer draw revenues from the former lands of the Catholic Church, then taxation would be increased. Thus there was ample support for James when in 1584 he declared himself head of church and state, and duly appointed bishops responsible to the King as moderators of Presbyteries. In this arrangement Falkirk was made part of the Bishopric of Edinburgh. By the time that Alexander Livingstone died in 1622 an observer might have been pardoned for thinking that the problem of the kirk had been resolved. In Falkirk the Kirk was apparently firmly established as a unit of James VI's episcopal system with a fanatical episcopalian, William Annand, as minister, and the Earl of Linlithgow of strong episcopalian persuasion as patron.

However when his son, Alexander, succeeded to the estates he was immediately faced along with the other great landlords of Scotland with a far from settled situation. In 1626 the new King, Charles I, proceeded to estrange the two most influential sections of Scottish society, the landlords and the Kirk. The title deeds of all lands acquired since the Reformation were to be examined by royal officials and it was patent that the King was seeking additional revenues to provide stipends for the ministry and for the establishment of parish schools. The landlord felt threatened. It would appear that sixty years of ownership were not enough to provide security of tenure.

At the same time Charles talked of conformity in religion in England and Scotland and it was clear that he meant that the Anglican form of worship should supersede the Presbyterian religion. Ministers could hear confession. A service book was to be introduced even if it had not the sanction of the General Assembly. Charles was named, "Head of the Church."

In Falkirk the national uproar against bishops and the new liturgy resulted in 1638 in Margaret Clelland being called to "answer for casting stones at the Bischope of Galloway." In March the schoolmaster and Session Clerk, John Dischingtoun was given the "soume of 50s" for preparing a copy of the Confession of Faith which thereafter was subscribed by "the Parson, gentlemen, elders and honest men of the parochin." In the same year the National Covenant declared that its signatories would not accept the innovations until they had been approved of by the General Assembly and Parliament. The General Assembly then proceeded to demolish the whole episcopal system.

This challenge to royal power could not be ignored. The King prepared to invade Scotland. A Covenanting army rushed to arms. One of its foremost leaders who had had a distinguished career in the Thirty Years War in Germany was the younger son of Alexander, First Earl of Linlithgow. In 1633 this Sir James Livingstone, Lord Almond purchased the estates of Callendar from his elder brother, Alexander, who now made his chief residence Midhope Castle in West Lothian. Thus the new laird of Callendar and feudal superior of Falkirk took up residence in time to be drawn into a civil war. On the outbreak of the Bishops' Wars he recruited a contingent of men from the Parish of Falkirk to join the battalions of the Kirk, who under the command of Alexander Leslie soon defeated the King. Renewed fighting broke out in 1640 and the Lord Livingstone was promoted second-in-command.

In February, 1640 the Kirk Session intimated from the pulpit that "dreilling begins to be practised upon Fryday com eight days." It also appealed for "ane voluntarie contributione for the present service of the warre." The Covenanters were again successful. Charles made peace with the Scots and Livingstone returned to Falkirk with a new title, Earl of Callendar. The future of Presbyterianism seemed assured.

The very success of the Scots was indirectly their undoing. Faced with the need to raise the very substantial sum of money demanded by the Covenanters as reparations, Charles had to summon his English

Parliament which he had managed to do without for eleven years. Parliament thereupon reduced the King's power to such an extent that he determined to risk life and crown in a further resort to war. The Scottish covenanters could not but be alarmed. Should Charles win would he use his victorious armies to replant episcopacy in Scotland? So when the English Parliament appealed for Scottish help, the leaders of the Kirk were not slow to respond. They would save Presbyterianism by saving the English Parliament, demanding as the price of their support the promise that after victory a unified Presbyterian Church would be set up in both kingdoms. The leaders of Parliament and every Scot would be asked to sign the Solemn League and Covenant in these terms.

In the Minutes of Kirk Session of 31st March, 1643 it was ordered that "on Sunday when the Covenant salbe subscryved, the persounes following sall attend the several parts of the Kirk." There follows the names of elders who would ensure that the covenant set on a table before the pulpit was dutifully signed, those failing so to do being classed as "enemies to religioune" and being made to face censure from the church and punishment from the civil authorities.

And so Falkirk once more went to war. "All fencible men from sixteen to sixty are to be in readiness to tak the field when ordered." This pulpit proclamation gave notice of conscription. It was "ordainit ane collectioune for schoulders claithes . . . and a relief granted to widows, orphans and to mutilated sojers." Lady Pantasken claimed aid for her husband "killed on the public service."

The Earl of Callendar with a contingent from Falkirk joined the Covenanters. On this occasion he did not enjoy the highest office for he had denied support to the Earl of Argyle, "King Campbell" in his claim to be Captain-General North of the Forth. Callendar and his men fought well at Marston Moor and helped in the capture of York. In 1645 he was in charge of the force which took Carlisle. In the following year the war was over, the King surrendering to the Scots at Newark.

A few months later Callendar met with the King and a charter dated at Newcastle on 22nd July, 1646 is another milestone in the advance of the Livingstone family and in the civic history of Falkirk, for it created Falkirk a Burgh of Regality with all the extended privileges involved.

The new Earl of Callendar, however, had not long to enjoy his new possessions and dignity. The generals of the New Model Army were unwilling to permit Presbyterianism to be established in England as promised by Parliament. Charles saw the prospect of salvaging his fortunes. He entered negotiations with the disappointed Scots promising to establish Presbyterianism in both kingdoms for a trial period of three years if they would assist him in overthrowing his

33

enemies. The limited period offered in this so-called "Engagement" did not appeal to most leaders in Scotland. However, some Scots including the Earl of Callendar and 73 men from Falkirk took up arms on the king's behalf. The bungling of the Duke of Hamilton, the Scottish leader, and the ruthless efficiency of the New Model Army under Cromwell routed the Scots. The detachment from Falkirk, exasperated at the conduct of their incapable general and spurning the opportunity of ignominious surrender, broke through the encircling English troops and forced their way home. The Earl of Callendar fled to Holland, while those who returned to Falkirk faced the censure of the leading party in the Kirk. Presbytery indeed sent a deputation to examine minister and elders of the Parish Kirk "for notice is taken of how far the gentlemen of the paroch of Falkirk were accessorie to the late unlawful engagement." They declared that Falkirk was a stronghold of "The Malignants" and noted that those who marched with the Earl of Callendar had been "admonished by the Session but had made no public repentance." The minister, Mr Edward Wright, was suspended.

Falkirk unfortunately had not seen the end of war. After Charles I had been executed in 1649 his son arrived in Scotland and agreed to take the Covenant. Cromwell, appreciating the danger, unleashed his army on Scotland. After his fortunate victory at Dunbar in 1650, the English army came to Falkirk in pursuit of the royal force encamped at the Torwood.

Drama for a brief moment centred on Callendar House where a small garrison refused to surrender. After a final summons was scornfully rejected the guns were wheeled into position and the issue swiftly decided. A brief bombardment brought a breach in the walls through which the English stormed.

A letter from Cornet Baynes dated 19th July, 1651 gives a short account of the incident. "From the camp near Kallender House . . . we advanced again to Fawkirk near to Torwood. We have been here four nights. Upon Tuesday last about sunset after we had made a breach upon Kallendar House even in the face of the enemy we stormed it and lost a captain of foot, our gunner Robert Hargreave of your troop and 2 or 3 private soldiers. More were slain in the storm. We slew the enemy about 50 persons, and such as had quarter given them were most of them wounded. Little was taken in the house except horses and cattle of the country people."

General Monck repaired the House and for a time resided there. One of the stairs in the House is even to this day called Monck's staircase. Falkirk was made to learn the woe that comes to the conquered. The minutes of Kirk Session note the losses of corn, cattle and sheep suffered by parishioners. One countryman reports

"4 aickers of land, 30 sheep, 2 ky ane quoy and ane stirk" forfeited to the English. The Kirk was a dormitory for English troops and their horses grazed in the kirkyard. In 1655 when times were more settled those "whos seats within the kirk was broken down in the tyme of trubles" were told to "come and own them." There were, too, frequent complaints that women of the town were too free with the English garrison and ill-tempered brawls with men of the town were not unusual.

With the Restoration of Charles II in 1660 the Earl of Callendar returned to Falkirk. He was, however, never again a prominent figure. Though he was one of the fourteen nobles who bore the remains of the great Marquis of Montrose to their place of burial in St. Giles, he was normally content to seek the shadow. He was active, however, in rebuilding Callendar House and laying out the grounds in the manner he had seen in Holland. As a tribute to the town which had supported him in his more active days, he founded a hospital for the maintenance of four aged persons on a location between where now the Temperance Cafe stands and the Crown hotel.

Another token of thanksgiving was the building of the Cross Well on the South side of the High Street by the Steeple. The Earl thanked the citizens for their gallantry. He filled a goblet from the fountain and drank a toast "To the wives and bairns of Falkirk" which may well be the origin of the name which has remained with Falkirk folk thereafter.

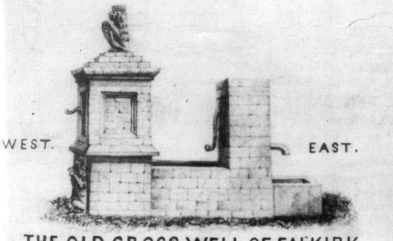

WEST.

EAST.

THE OLD CROSS WELL OF FALKIRK.

James Livingstone was childless. One of his earliest duties on his return was to will his estates and titles to his nephew, the second son of his elder brother, Alexander. The article so disposing of his properties is dated 29th May, 1663 though it did not become effective until 1672 when the old Earl was buried in the Parish Kirkyard. It is interesting because of the placenames contained in its list of properties and also for its reference to the new status of the burgh of Falkirk achieved in 1646:

"The lands, barony and castle of Callendar, the dominical lands of Ffalkirk with the strath forest of the same, the lands of Ffalkirk, the two Carmuirs, the two Auchingavels and Glen, Easter and Wester Jaws, Jawcraig, Bogtoun, Hallglens, Shielhill, Wallhill, Slamannan Muir, Levielands, Croft, Fidderal, with castle and towers. The lands of Callendar Mains and the strath forest of the same at the east end of the wood of Callendar, Hawglens, Wallhill, Easter and Wester Glens, Berriewaird, West end of Craigrige, Druncastlerige, Shielhill, Gremrige, Easter and Wester Jaws, Thresprige, Easter and Wester Auchingavens, Jawcraig, Swynerige, Blackfaulds, Beam Lochrige, Gremrige, Shortrige, Whyterashes, Howierige, Knows, Rigend, Kilbain, Blackhill, Jamie's Croft, the coal work of Ffalkirk, Easter Carmuirs, Bogtoun, Tamfourhill, Pairmeadows, Mill of Carmuirs, Lady'smylne with the whole town and lands of Ffalkirk. The lands of Slamannan Muir, Crosthill, Middlerig, Balcastle, Castlehill, Howehouse, Craigend, Parkshaw, Wester Dalwhairn, Bolwhatstone, the Easter and Wester Dykeheids, the Half Merk, with the right and patronage of the Kirk of Slamannan and the half of the town and lands of Stainehouse. The feu farms of Airth and Abbotshaugh, Beircrofts, Saltcoats, Hewick, Reidheugh, with annual rents to be uplifted yearly from the lands of Manuel and Quarrel and the full power of liberty to hold and appoint courts of Baillery and justiciary thereupon. The liberties and privileges of a harbour and station for ships upon lands of Dalderse contiguous to the waters of Carron for the transport of coals from Ffalkirk coal works to the sea. . . The land, barony and buildings of Hayning, Manuel, Parkhall, Hillside, Madiston (with the coals and coal heughs of the same) Gilmoirstoun, Niccoltoun, Gillandersland, Manuelrig, Gilmundieland, Easter and Wester Ballenbreich, mills of Manuel and Mallenbreich, with all the lands, mills, etc. of the barony of Hayning, the lands of Whyting, Walkemyletoun, Easter and Wester Tupeheids and Williamcraigs . . ."

"And erects, creates and incorporates the foresaid town and burgh of Falkirk with the whole bounds, parts and pendicles and pertinents thereof, into a whole and free burgh of regality to be called in all times coming the Burgh of Falkirk and with the power to the said Lord Livingstone to have and build a court and prison within the said burgh and liberties as well for the securing of all prisoners and malefactors and with the power to elect bailies and other magistrates and liberty to the burgesses of Falkirk to buy and sell wine, wax, salt, bread etc. with the pick and peill therein like any other free regality two weekly market days the one on Tuesday and the other on Friday and four fairs yearly . . ."

The new Earl after 1672 immediately brought trouble to town and district. Deeply covenanter by sympathy he quickly roused suspicion in the minds of the authorities. Royal troops were moved into the area on several occasions. In 1682 Alexander was finally stripped of his hereditary power of bailery and justiciary over the Sheriffdom of Stirling, his baronial power over Falkirk passing to the second son of the Third Earl of Linlithgow. Alexander died in 1685.

There is an oft repeated evaluation of the attitude of the people of Falkirk to religious unrest during the 17th century. This judgment has been formed because in the Minutes of Kirk Session protest is rare and business is mainly parochial. George Murray in his review of the Minutes states "the Falkirk Bairns must have been either very loyal subjects or had the happy knack of accommodating themselves to the usages of the time." "Immunity from ecclesiastical agitation appears to have been characteristic of Falkirk."

Enough has already been told of Falkirk's involvement in the national struggle between King and Kirk to make nonsense of these assertions. In a day when defiance of the establishment could well rank as treason, with minister and Kirk Session usually of episcopalian persuasion, it would have been surprising to find any criticism of monarch and church placed on record. When Episcopacy was re-established in 1660 it had been ordained that all ministers admitted after 1649 should seek presentation by the patron of their churches and then appointment by a bishop. 270 ministers refused and were expelled. These "outed" ministers began to hold field meetings. The authorities reacted strongly. Outed ministers could not live within twenty miles of their old parishes. Death was prescribed for any one preaching at a conventicle.

Falkirk was not free from this defiance of authority. In 1673 it was among the parishes reported to His Majesty's Commissioner for holding field meetings. In the Kirk Session minutes appears the injunction "that the minister should make publick intimatione that no persone should vage or goe in companie to the woode or any other place upone the Sabbath day." In 1674 masters were made responsible for the religious beliefs of their servants. Fines were imposed on those absent from worship on three consecutive Sundays. Such regulations give the lie to assertions that "periods of national excitement passed unheeded by Falkirk parishioners."

37

There is one further piece of evidence supporting the belief that there was at Falkirk an organised resistance to the Anglican Church. In 1687 the new Catholic monarch, James II, issued a Declaration of Liberty of Conscience giving relief from penal laws against any opponents of the Anglican Church. His idea was to smooth the path for Roman Catholics, but, profiting from this toleration, four Presbyterian ministers set up a Presbytery at Bo'ness outwith the influence of a Bishop. Almost at once "the people of Falkirk" applied for Presbyterian ministers to preach to them, indicating the presence of an already active Presbyterian community.

The succession of William of Orange brought an end to the century-old struggle, and though the new Earl of Callendar offered determined resistance to the appointment of a Presbyterian minister, the cause at length triumphed, but not before Presbytery, General Assembly, Privy Council and even the Scottish Parliament were involved.

The turn of the 18th century brought the long association of the Livingstone family with Falkirk to an end. The succession of James, Fifth Earl of Linlithgow and Fourth Earl of Callendar was a misfortune for his House. His decision to throw in his lot with the Old Pretender in 1715, and his commanding a squadron of horse at Sheriffmuir, led to his estates and titles being forfeit. The final severance of the Livingstone connection was however delayed. His daughter, Ann, was able to rent the House from the new owners, the York Building Company, and so for a time there was still a Livingstone at Callendar. In 1746, however, her husband supported Prince Charlie and paid the supreme penalty on Tower Hill. Thereafter the mourning widow turned her back forever on the house and parkland where for exactly four hundred years Livingstones had dwelled.

Callendar House About 1789

38

There is no record of the death of the last Earl of Callendar except that it was in 1725. Might he not, however, on his death-bed have contemplated the peculiar parallel between the fate of his dynasty and that of the ill-fated House of Stewart in whose cause he had dared and lost all? Remembering that the first Livingstone at Callendar had married Christiane the better to consolidate his newly acquired possessions and thinking of his own daughter, now the mere tenant of what he had once owned, might he not with justice have echoed the dying words of James V, "It cam wi' a lass; it'll gang wi' a lass"?

In 1783 at an auction held in Old Parliament Hall in Edinburgh, William Forbes purchased Callendar House. The first Forbes of Callendar had made a fortune out of his position of supplier to the Admiralty of all manner of products not least the anti-barnacle sheaths which earned him the nickname "Copperbottom Forbes." He was a shrewd businessman, and it was not long before he effected many changes in his new estates and set the pattern to his successors of active participation in local politics, in the parish kirk and in the economic development of the Falkirk area.

Such activity was not always popular. In 1797 in the Home Office Papers is recorded that "Mr Forbes's House at Callendar (one of the largest and best in Scotland) was sett fire to last night about seven by people supposed from Falkirk . . . and with some difficulty he made his

Callendar House today

39

escape in to an adjoining wood and so to Linlithgow with what was on his back only." It might well have been that the repressive government legislation of the time and the unsettled mood inspired by revolutionary events in France did as much to incite this demonstration as hostility to the new laird.

In the 19th century the House was much improved with the laying out of formal gardens, an artificial canal and the remodelling of the upper portion of the House to give the appearance of a French chateau. Wings were added and a new porch and entrance hall. A driveway, rarely used, was cut through the Antonine Wall out to the Callendar Road. It is said to provide an impressive approach for a visit of Queen Victoria who, in the event, did not after all arrive. In the kitchen was installed a huge mechanical spit made in the Carron Iron Company, one of two, the other being supplied to George IV at Brighton.

In the 1960s Falkirk rediscovered Callendar Estate when in 1963 it was purchased by the Town Council. Down came the encircling walls and some of the most tastefully designed high flats in the country rose above lawns, gardens and sports grounds. As residential area and playground, Callendar Estate has a secure future partnership with Falkirk. Not so, unfortunately, the building which is the centre-piece of the complex. Much infected with dry rot and woodworm, Callendar House requires very sizeable sums to be spent before it can fulfil any of the many roles in which it has been cast — museum, social centre, hotel, conference centre, flats. Even the ghosts of Mary and Darnley, Elizabeth of Bohemia and James VI, Monck and Cromwell, Bonnie Prince Charlie and a host of the nation's most famous sons, are not enough to ensure conservation.

Once before Callendar House lay under the auctioneer's hammer. Then it was merely a matter of change of ownership. It had yet many years to serve family and community. Now again its future rests with the caller, this time the choice being between survival and extinction. "Going, going . . ." Bearing in mind how little history in stone remains within the burgh and the singular historical heritage encased within its walls, it will surely be a tragedy if the hammer should sound out "Gone."

CHAPTER V

SOCIAL WELFARE AND TYRANNY:
Kirk and Society in the 17th and 18th centuries.

During the 17th and 18th centuries, the prominence of the Parish Kirk in the everyday life of Falkirk did not rest with its dominating position on that mound above the town. In a remarkable, and to our generation, inexplicable way, it was able to impose its authority on the whole pattern of living, invading the privacy of the home, dictating which pastimes and recreations were permissible, denying personal liberty by implanting a harsh and often unhealthy discipline on all who lived within the jurisdiction of its court. Though some of its ordinances may be construed as the first stumbling steps towards social welfare, the main effect was tyranny rather than benevolence, intolerance rather than charity, the very negation of that virtue named as greatest by the very Founder of the Faith.

One most important benefit provided by the Kirk was the foundation of a parish school. Though the Presbyterial visitation of 1628 makes no reference to a school at Falkirk, by 1632 the Kirk Session Minute states that "John Dischingtoun has been appoyntit Sessioune Clerk" and describes him as "schoolmaster at Falkirk." There is no accurate description of the earliest school except that the building in which it was housed required renovation. The school day was long. "The six hour bell summoned ye bairnies to the schule" and except for an hour at breakfast and an hour at dinner, school continued until six in the evening. Saturday was a full school day. By 1689, however, there was a relaxation in hours. School commenced at seven o'clock in the summer and nine o'clock in winter, and there was a half day on Saturdays.

The main group of children catered for were the six to nine year olds. In March 1644 it was "ordainit that all ye bairnies within the toune who are past six yeirs of age should cum to the common schule." Attendance was not, however, compulsory for duties in the fields and in the home took precedence.

The salaries paid to masters were not large. Mr James Levingstoun, appointed in 1644 was paid "fourtie pounds" together with certain

41

rents. A pound was the equivalent of present-day 6p and at no time until the late 18th century was any master paid more than £12. In addition school fees of 5p per pupil per quarter could be levied. The Session however made the qualification that if "there wer any whose parents wer not able to pay in that case he should teach them gratis." The schoolmaster added to his salary by what he earned as Session Clerk, Registrar, and by certain casual payments which came his way. For instance the fighting cocks reared by the boys to fight just before Lent became his property when they were killed. Less to be envied was the assistant master. In 1644 "Robert Wingzet agreed with the Sessioune to tak tryell for a quarter of ane yeir haveing ane sixpence for everie bairn that was within the schule that tyme."

The Session was careful that no school was set up that might compete with the parish school over which they had control. Certain private establishments which tried to open were firmly told to desist, the one exception being in the 1640s when a female teacher was permitted "to teach the lassies weaveing and sewing" but on no account "the reading."

One must not be misled into the belief that the creation of a "toun schule" in Falkirk meant the fashioning of a new society. The population continued to wallow in a trough of ignorance, superstition and illiteracy, for in spite of the ordinances of the Session attendance at school was irregular. In any case a school and a schoolmaster do not necessarily add up to education, and there was constant difficulty in obtaining men of scholarship and character to be teachers. Lack of books, paper and even desks little concerned the only people who had it in their power to bring improvement. The local heritors were ever mindful of their purses and paid out as little as conscience and the Acts of Parliament would permit, leaving the schoolmaster a mere pittance and the scholars sprawling on straw-covered floors, coughing in the reek of the peat fire which was their only warmth amid the draughts which blew in through broken windows, cracked walls and leaking thatch.

By 1800, Falkirk like many other Scottish towns had divided its parish school into two separate institutions. There was foremost the grammar school where a strongly academic education was provided — English, the Classics, Mathematics, History, Geography. There was also the more lowly English school where the main components of the instruction were reading, writing and arithmetic.

One serious intrusion into the private lives of parishioners in the 17th century was the Kirk's insistence on family religious exercise. Heads of the household were ordered to ensure that morning and night their families met for prayer and to sing psalms. The Ten Commandments, the Apostles' Creed and the Lord's Prayer were to be learned by heart. Indeed in 1648 it was ordained that "non sall be married bott such as can say the comon beliefs and the Lord's Prayer."

Tight controls were enforced on those who wished to avail themselves of the services of the Kirk for special occasions. Baptisms were not to be made an excuse for revelry and there are frequent complaints against those who allowed "fiddlin at Christenin." In 1618 the Session ordained that no banns could be called until both parties came before the Session and declared their intention to marry and put up £5 as surety of good faith. Marriages had to take place within forty days of the promise being given. The practice in the early reformed church was to have weddings solemnised before the congregation on Sunday morning, but the temptation to celebrate over-heartily on the Sabbath led to a change. In 1647 it was ordained "that ther will be no marriages bott on Thursdays." The Session were particularly concerned about "penny weddings" which were a cause of "drunkenness and debauche." In 1647 "it was ordainit that there be no pyping at brydalls." The number of guests were restricted to "no moir nor sixteen persones on ilk syd." Even a century later the Session continued to wage this particular battle. "Taking into their consideratione the great abuses that are and may be committed at penny weddynges by pypers playing persounes to the church to be married and when they are coming from the church to their homes and also playing to people to dance, therefore the Session appoyntes their officer to cite James Scheddings and George Monteith, pypers, against thir nixt meeting."

Funerals were also subject to strict regulations. The lyke-wake was forbidden because watchers demanded frequent refreshment which all too often resulted in drunken revelry. There were to be no funeral feasts for the same reason. In the 17th century no services were allowed over the open grave. The burial of corpses within the church was stopped and as the century advanced tombstones became increasingly a feature of the churchyard.

On one tragic occasion burial in the churchyard was refused. The visitation of plague to Scotland in 1645 struck fear at the hearts of most communities. Falkirk did its best to avoid contact with diseased areas. No one was permitted to travel to Glasgow. "No shearers are to be hyred without ane pass." The town was however too centrally placed to avoid contamination. Many Falkirk men were serving with the Covenanting armies on the Borders where the plague was very rife. The inevitable happened.

"Margaret Kincaid to keep within doores till the clenser come heir." "No foul house to be cleansed until the clean houses are cleansed." Those stricken were given the not altogether hopeful advice to close their houses "until the change of the moon."

The victims of the Plague were buried in what became known as the Pest Graves on Graham's Muir. Round the graves which were marked with flat stones was built a dyke by John Tennant concerning whom the Session Minute of 3rd October, 1647 reports, "The dyke about the deid in ye Graham's Muir is sufficiently wrought and therfor it is ordainit to give the said John Tenant 12 lb."

For many years after 1647 this spot which lay close to the junction of present-day Russel Street and George Street was shunned by all. Cattle which inadvertently strayed near the Pest Graves were milked and the milk thrown away for a full fortnight after their contact. In the early 19th century, however, inhibitions were swept away. A grazier called Dunn took down the walls and allowed his beasts to graze freely. Soon the land which belonged to Dr Meek who gave his name to Meek's Road was bought by builders and the tangible evidence of one of Falkirk's greatest disasters was finally erased.

One of the most worthy functions of the Kirk was poor relief. There was a poor box at the door of the Kirk. Endowments and money willed to the Kirk helped swell this never adequate fund. Relief was reserved to "sic as are beggaris in the paroche and has the parish token." This token permitted the holder to beg freely throughout the parish. A description of the 18th century Beggar's Badge is contained in the Session Minutes of 1725. It was described as "a pewter mettall round to the bulk of half-a-crown piece marked with F.K.K. with the top of the Kirk Steeple above." At Falkirk beggars were paid on the first Thursday of each month. Though it was expected that recipients would collect personally "yheir allotment," in cases of illness elders were detailed to make payment in the homes. The Session was ever anxious to keep down the number of claims upon the Poor Fund. There are regular attacks against "vagabond beggars" and on those who harbour them. Newcomers to the parish were closely questioned for fear that they might become a burden on the Fund. Highlanders were not to be received "under any circumstances." In 1687 the Kirk Session and heritors "mett that they bring exact lists of theire owne poore within the paroch of Falkirk." Thereafter they agreed "that the heretors put out of there bounds stranger beggars and uther idle persounes that are burdensome to the paroch." Constables were appointed to cast out stranger beggars. Public intimation was made at the Cross of Falkirk that all persons not authorised should "depart from ye toune within twenty-four houris and from ye landward part of ye paroch within a weeke." Though effective for more than a generation, these precautions in defence of the poor fund had to be repeated on several occasions and there are regular references to "randie beggars" who were unlicensed being despatched to the Correction House at Stirling.

In 1643 Gilbert Blakhal, an English traveller in Scotland, inserted in his diary a short description of a Sunday morning in Falkirk. "I was mounted on my horse by the break of day, and passing by the Falkirk, a place where Wallace resorted oft, I did see the country people whigging their mares to be tymeously at the kirk as if they had been running for a pryse. They passed me bidding me spurre my horse to communicate with them." The haste to be punctually in their places was reflected in the bustle of the town dwellers for with elders placed at the Kirk doors to note latecomers, there was incentive enough.

At the Kirk door stood that inevitable band of penitents in "sack claithes" or "hair goons." All through the long period of psalm singing they would stand barelegged and sometimes barefoot no matter what the weather until summoned at the third bell to take their places on "The Pillar," a raised platform in full view of the congregation. After 1695 they were denied the slight comfort of being placed a distance from the pulpit, the minister of the time complaining that "the pillar is at so great a distance from the pulpit and so darklie situat that rebukes given to persounes on the pillar are exposed to contempt." The pillar was then moved centrally..

Over 90% of the business of the Kirk Session before 1750 was concerned with summoning the "guilty" to answer for some action or omission, the questioning of the accused, the resummoning of those who failed to appear at the first citation.

Among the many offences none appears more regularly than Sabbath breaking. Bad enough to be late for Kirk. Worse to be absent without good cause. But to defy the rules of the Kirk in what constituted proper Sunday conduct was certain to incur the dread summons to "compcir." Much of what was then considered improper behaviour would by 20th century standards be classified as in the worst traditions of Puritanism: "Idly gazing from windows," "walking fast on the Lord's Day," "loiteringe upone ye Sabbath," "walking in the fields," "hiring shearers," "handling corne," "spreading muck," "shoeing a horse," "baking," "picking pease," "grindin wi' a hand-mill," "yoking a pleuch," "carting divots," "spreading webs o' clothis," "climbing craws nests," "salmon fishing," "carrying water from ye well," and many other similar transgressions. "Drinking on ye Sabbath" was viewed with especial disapproval. "In time of sermoun," elders were despatched to seek out "persouns drinking" either in the ale houses of the town or in that favourite resort of those who acquired a weekend thirst, Beancross. Even the privacy of one's own home might be invaded by one of the "collectors." Numerous devices were employed to evade the vigilance of the Church authorities, not least ingenious being the activities of John Wilson who blood let on the Sabbath. The fact that "the said John Wilson" invariably sustained his patient with a dram made him an ever popular alternative to attendance at the Kirk.

It was not, however, over the Sabbath Day only that the Session claimed oversight of personal conduct. Its watchful and meddlesome presence interposed itself in all manner of everyday situations. "Brawling," "cheating," "lying," "scolding," "dancing promisky (i.e., with women) to fiddle and pypes," "being late from his father's house" were other offences brought before the bar of the church court. "Sweiring" is a constant matter of concern. In 1668 there was a condemnation of "the horrible and unchristian life of the fleshers of the town, profaning the Lord's name by cursing and sweiring." Elders were appointed to visit the Fleshmarket and report on the amount of swearing to be heard.

Gambling was of course under severe censure. The most popular local game in the seventeenth century was "playing the goose." "John Watt confesst his profanation of the Sabathe by playing the goose on the Claydinges in tyme of the afternoune sermoun." The Claydinges or Claydens was the area above the East Bridge at the bottom of East Bridge Street for many years the playground of Falkirk. The Goose was played on a board numbered off into sixty-three squares in a spiral with No. 63 the open space in the centre. Each player threw two dice in turn, adding the numbers together and moving a counter according to what was thrown. Every four or five squares there was marked a goose which allowed the player to double his score. Hazards were placed along the route. At Square 5 was a bridge for which a toll was exacted. Square 19 showed an alehouse where one lost two throws. At Square 30 there was a fountain where one must pay for washing. Square 42 was a labyrinth which led back to Square 23. Square 52 was a prison where one must remain until someone threw the same number which had landed the player in jail. Square 58 was the worst hazard of all for it was The Grave and meant that one must start again. Square 61 showed a goblet for whose tasting one must pay. All charges were set in the centre and the player who ultimately reached Square 63 exactly collected all. If one's throw took one too far, the additional numbers were counted backwards. In view of the frequent punishments from the Church authorities which the Goose brought to those who were tempted to enjoy its uncertainties, it seems strange that among the hazards on the board there did not appear the menacing figure of the prowling elder.

"Flyting women" are notable for the frequency with which they intrude into Kirk Session business. Menfolk of those days had a real safeguard against the nagging wife for she could be summoned to face the censure of the Kirk. In the worst cases the offender was ordered to be fitted with the branx, a device muzzling its wearer by an iron leaf being placed over the tongue. Whether moved to repentance by this most effective headpiece, she was at least for the time condemned to silence.

Then there were the witches. In 1622 the Kirk Session Minutes report "The which day compeirit John Wairden, Younger, Webster in Falkirk, which being the day of his marriage and with him George Wilson, Webster, that he shall underly the discipline and censure of the kirk for his going to Stirling and consulting Janet Andersoune, chairmer and witch anent the seiknes of Carra Wairden, his sister." One Falkirk witch recorded in 1622 was Margaret Darnformer, but her fate is unreported. It was a cruel time when superstitious fear condemned many an unfortunate body to an awesome death for no greater reason than looking the part or uttering an unguarded threat. Burning before or after strangulation or drowning were the usual penalties. In this climate of almost hysterical dread of the dark forces it was a temptation to pay off personal scores by levelling charges of witchcraft against an enemy. Janet Buchanan in her private feud with Christian Watson all but succeeded, several witnesses perjuring themselves by complaining of injuries willed upon them by Christian. However she, too, was not without friends and at her trial produced so many upright and worthy citizens who being "sworne to depone and declair upone thir conscience gine they knew anie presumptiounes or appeirances of witchcraft to the said Christiane Watsoune deponed all in ane voice that they knew nothing in hir but honestie."

It was now Janet who was on trial. She was sentenced to "mak publik repentance for six severall Sabathes in sackclaith and to stand in the said habit at the church doore ilk day of the said six Sabathes from the ringing of the first bell to the sermoun . . . and thereafter to cum with the said habit into the church and remane there the tyme of the sermoun and upone the last of the said Sabathes in face of the congregation she shall be requyrit by the minister to humblie confess and acknowledge hir filthie and abominable fault to the glorie of God and exempill of otheris." Janet did not learn by her punishment and in 1627 she was condemned to the cruel sentence of banishment. In those days when all parishes were intent on keeping down the number of people within the parish bounds requiring poor relief such a punishment meant that an outcast would be driven from place to place without respite. Perhaps it was this treatment that brought her back to Falkirk, but no compassion awaited her. On 6th January, 1627 the Session issued what it must have considered to be its last word: "As Janet Buchanan was by ane former act set dune for her godless, wicked and prophane life . . . and thairfor was ordaint by the civil magistrate to be banished . . . nonetheless the said Janet has

47

had residence in the toune since and is yet found to live as wickedlie in hir lyfe and conversatioune . . . and because she can find nane to be caution for hir obedience the minister and elderis with the advyce and consent of the bailies have thought mete to release her forth and ordaines her to remove herself out of the toun and paroche within the space of fourtie dayes . . . and not to be seen here in no tyme cuming hereafter with certificatione to be made to her gin she fails she shall be stoned and burned." Janet must have been a rash or desperate woman to have returned with such a sentence hanging over her head, but return she did only to meet an even more determined Session which warned her that if she fail again to betake herself forth of the town and parish she would suffer death by drowning. Thereafter Janet disappears from the records.

The Kirk Session viewed with disfavour the superstitious visitation of wells, whose waters were supposed to have magical healing properties. Christ's Well, later known as Greenhorn's Well in Gartcows was a favourite. The ritual on such a visit was not to speak on the way, to leave some money and a napkin, and not to lay down the vessel containing the water until Falkirk was reached. Another popular well was at Airth. "Margaret Walker went to the well at Airth to fetch water to Rob. Cowie and when sche com thair sche laid doon moneys in God's name and ane napkin in Rob. Cowie's name." "Bessie Thomson left money theirat and efter the can was fillet with water they keepit it untuiching the ground till they cam hame."

Immorality was one of the principal transgressions dealt with by the Session. At almost every diet over two hundred years there are cases of young men and women brought to answer for "fornication" or "adultery" or even "bygames." Even the hasty marriage was not enough to save the humiliation demanded by the fathers of the Kirk, who were expert in calculating how long the parents of each child had been legally joined in wedlock. To study the proceedings of the Court of the Kirk is to be aware not only of the futility of the over-zealous and excessive interference of the Kirk in the ordinary lives of the parishioners, for the number of offences varies hardly at all throughout the two centuries, but also of the existence of human frailty as a constant element in society, the characteristic of no one age.

Yet this cruel, relentless tyranny continued and produced frequent suicides, murdered bairns and unhappy victims fleeing the country. There is something tragic in the self-righteous horror voiced by the Session at the "murdered infant found in water of Carron" and the diligence with which the Session appointed elders and midwives to make a speedy search "both in town and landward" with the prayer that "by the good providence of God directing them the blood guilty may be discovered" when part of the blame for such a crime rested assuredly on the petty and unchristian rule of the church authorities themselves.

But the end was in sight. The rising middle class and the artisan class engaged in the new industries that appeared in the second half of the 18th century refused any longer to brook such interference. The breakaway from the Established Church reduced uniform discipline. By 1760 the custom had appeared of writing to the Session acknowledging guilt rather than appearing in person. Even more defiant was the young woman who retorted to the representative of the Session sent to summon her to answer for her illegitimate child that "as neither he nor the session would bring up the child" neither he nor the Session had any business with it. Sounding like the obituary of a passing age there is the rather plaintive note in the Session entry "that there are little hopes of getting him (another offender) before any Church Court." Before long the outright rebel declined to submit to the "judicatory" of the Session. For a time yet the Kirk Session continued to browbeat the meek and timid, but there was no longer an answer to the person who would challenge it to do its worst. An extraordinary period of unwarranted interference in everyday living had come to a close, not least remarkable in that its end was so long delayed.

CHAPTER VI

BAPTISM AND GROWING PAINS

The granting of the Charter to Falkirk as a Burgh of Barony in 1600 might appear to mark the civic baptism of the town. There is no doubt that the event brought important advantages to the community. With the Charter came rights and privileges for long jealously guarded by the merchants and craftsmen of the royal burgh of Stirling, anxious to avoid competition from a less elevated but commercially dangerous neighbour. Permission to hold weekly markets and annual fairs, to sell produce hitherto reserved for the royal burghs, to work at crafts and trades for long monopolised by the craft gilds of Stirling, all brought the prospect of prosperity and diversification of employment. The erection of a Baron's Court, even though under the authority of the Sheriff, gave an increased status and dignity which Falkirk had not enjoyed since it first grew up round its mottled kirk.

In 1646 Falkirk became a Burgh of Regality which separated the Baron's Court from the jurisdiction of the Sheriff. It was allowed to have a Tolbooth for the imprisonment of criminals. The records of this court parade the minor offences which came within its authority, but serious offenders were still passed to Stirling for trial and sentence. Among the most common wrangles in the court were the positioning of march stones, the boundary markers between rigs in the open fields of those days. There were, too, numerous cases concerning the gathering of peats and firewood. The court drew up the regulations governing the keeping of cattle in houses and how they were to be herded to the town moor. In 1642 it was "ordainit that the hail indwellers within the toun of Falkirk quha hathe ony ky put thame to ane common herd under the pain of 20 shillings," no doubt a regulation intended to dissuade townsfolk from letting their animals stray, a practice which frequently led to damage being done to standing crops in the unfenced fields of the time. The cowherd of Falkirk was ordered to drive the cattle to the moor sounding his horn every day at four in the morning to call them forth from their owners' homes. Cattle were to be grazed until 11 a.m. and then driven back to their stalls until 2 in the afternoon when they were again rounded up and returned to pasture until sunset. Should the cowherd fail to be vigilant he was to be fined 6s. 8d. His wages were laid down by the court. "The owner of ilk kow that sall feid upon the common muirs of Falkirk to pay the commonherd weeklie 1s."

After 1646 four fairs were permitted annually. Two markets were held weekly on Tuesdays and Fridays, and the commercially astute were not slow in recognising the potential financial rewards that might come from controlling the tolls and market dues allowed by the burgh court. For a time the royal burghs tried to obstruct Falkirk's freedom of trade in certain items, but the breach had been made and by 1700 Falkirk traders were openly selling corn, oatmeal, cattle, sheep, wool, woollens, stockings, coal, salt, herrings, hides, fish, wax, and wines, and ironically at the same time resisting the sale of these goods in the small communities in the vicinity.

Another development strenuously opposed by the royal burghs was the right of the burgesses of Falkirk to engage in certain skilled trades. Burgess tickets were issued:

"The second day of September in the year of God sixteen hundred and three score and nineteen years, the quhilk day ane noble and potent Earle Alexander, Earle of Callender, Lord Livingstone of Almond and Ffalkirk freilie receives and admits Andrew Hutton, wright of Ffalkirk to libertie and freadome of ane neighbour and burges within the burgh of Ffalkirk with power to him to bruik joyse and use and exerce the haill liberties, priveleges and immunities pertaining yrto, siclyke and als frielie in all respects as oyr neighbour and burges may exerce and use within the said burghe of barronie and regalitie in tyme comeing; in suae far as concerneth the said noble and potent Earle his laws, present liberties yrof allenerlie venting and running of wyne being alwayes excepted and reserved heirof, and with this speciall and express provisione that the said Andrew Hutton shall use noe trade nor calling but onlie his own trade of wright and noe other . . ."

It was inevitable that as the number of tradesmen increased they began to draw together into gilds. The rights and powers of these gilds were recognised by the Baron in a number of charters, typical of which is the following:

"The first Julie in the year of God sixteen hundred and four score years and nine, We, Alexander, Earle of Callender, Lord Livingstone of Almond and Falkirk and lord of the burgh of barony and regality thereof do by these presents give full power warrant and commission to the hammermen, burgesses of the burgh of Falkirk to visit and sicht baith fair and mercat day all iron and pewther work that comes to be sold thereintill by any persons who are not burgesses and inhabitants within the said town and to exact and gait paid from

51

each of the said persons ilk fair day two shillings Scots and also fyne each person that brings insufficient iron or pewther work to be sold in the said fairs or mercats according as they have been in use sua to do in tyme past; and that each pewtherer shall pay two shillings Scots for each day that they shall set up or sell pewther work within the said town; and that no iron work shall be sold off ane fair or mercat day without the trades' leave; and with power to the said hammermen to chuyse their own deacon of trade . . . And in case any fault be committed by the said hammermen within the said town through insufficiency of their bound work to be made by them the said deacon shall fyne them according to the custom formerly used . . . and that each prentice that shall be bound to the said trade shall pay into the box-master thirtie shillings Scots and each journeymen six shillings eight pennies Scots . . . All things we will and consent to be done, performed and obeyed according as the said hammermen and their predecessors have been in use to do in any tyme past within the said toune and according to the former rights granted by our predecessors to them yreof . . ."

Though there were many valuable side-benefits for Falkirk from the burghal status acquired in 1600, its citizens had long to wait for any distinctive change in the pattern of local government. No progress or improvement could be initiated without the authority and consent of the feudal superior whose main concern was more frequently the restriction of expenditure than the common good. On numerous occasions the absence of the Earl on national or personal business delayed consideration of most pressing matters. Even more upsetting to the smoothness of the path towards efficient local management was the forfeiture in 1716 of Livingstone's titles. The regality came to an end and with it any semblance of unified control. The status of Falkirk vis-a-vis Stirling was reduced. It may or may not be true that a deputation of Stirling merchants joyfully cast down the mercat cross of Falkirk in 1716, in anticipation of a reversal to their previous dominance. Certainly the corporate life of Falkirk was seriously retarded for close on a century and a half, effective local government during those years passing into the hands of two bodies which emerged in the 17th century.

The first of these was the Stentmasters. Sometime in the 17th century a group of men called the Stentmasters were made responsible for the gathering of local dues on behalf of the Earl. There is no record until 1777 of the composition of this body. In that year there were 28 members, 4 elected by the merchant gild, 4 by "the pairts of the toun," i.e., the main districts of Falkirk — East Port, West Port, Vicar's Loan and Randygate, and the remaining 20 by the trade gilds— hammermen, wrights, weavers, whipmen, fleshers, shoemakers, masons, tailors, bakers and brewers. The election was held annually and there appears to have been no marked rigidity in the numbers appointed for in certain years there were 30 members and occasionally three of one trade were picked to compensate for another trade having no members.

The main interest of the Stentmasters was the upkeep of public property which in those days amounted to the Steeple, the fire engine and the water supply. They were responsible for raising money for the infrequent cleansing of the streets and half the lighting of the town. The manner of gathering the money was peculiar. It was not based on the holding of property. Stentmasters would consider each citizen's occupation and fix on some sum which they thought he might be able to pay. If he refused the Stentmasters had no jurisdiction to recover the money. When the exchequer was empty a new set of Stentmasters took over the burden. The officer engaged to make the actual collection was allowed 3d. out of every pound collected. He called only three times and if payment was refused no further action was taken. The lowest rate levied was 10½d. for a working man, and the highest a few pounds for the best off citizen. Little wonder then that the Town's finances were never adequate and always chaotic.

There were occasions when civic pride outweighed considerations of economy. In 1697 William Stevenson, mason, was given the task of replacing "the ruinous steeple" which had served the town since the 16th century. Unfortunately no description of this earliest building remains. The second Steeple was an imposing edifice entered by a flight of steps which jutted out across the High Street. During the 18th century a clock was fitted into the tower. The lack of accuracy of the clocks which have counted the passing hours for successive generations of Falkirk citizens has been the subject of much banter and not a little annoyance. One of the oldest prints of the High Street shows one of Falkirk's clockmakers standing in the doorway of his shop shielding his eyes to ensure that his charge was not lapsing into any fickle behaviour. A weathercock topped an elaborate tower in which the local jail was placed. There are frequent references to wrongdoers being lodged in the Tolbooth of Falkirk.

In 1801 Mr William Glen of Forganhall was given permission by Forbes of Callendar to use "the cellar by the ground floor or storey of the steeple in the street of Falkirk" provided that he did not "at any time hereafter deepen the said cellar or ground floor or in anywaise alter or weaken the walls on which the steeple is built or adjoining walls or do anything that may otherwise injure the Steeple."

Despite his assurance Glen did alter the cellar and shortly afterwards alarm was expressed at the state of the building. In 1803 it was

The Steeple 1697-1804

considered in "danger of collapse," and in order to avoid "threat to life and limb it was cast to the ground." Thus for ten years Falkirk was without its most prominent landmark. In the agitation to restore Falkirk's former glory, the Stentmasters took a leading part.

FALKIRK, 17th April, 1812.

Sir,

The Inhabitants of the Town of FALKIRK propose to build a New Steeple this Summer, in the Market place, where the Old Steeple stood, and in order to render it of as much utility as possible, not only to the Inhabitants of Falkirk, but also to the Public at large, in this District of the County, there are to be three Prison-Rooms in it for the purpose of confining Strolling Vagrants, and people who commit petty crimes. The necessity of having such places of confinement in this large and populous

54

district must appear evident to every person who has resided any length of time either in the Town or neighbourhood.

As the Building will be of public utility not only from the prison rooms it contains but also by having a Clock and Bell in it, it is expected that the Landed proprietors, Merchants, Farmers, &c. in the Eastern District of Stirling-Shire will Subscribe liberally to such a laudable and useful undertaking; without which it is feared, it may not be carried into execution.

In the course of a few days you will be waited upon with a Subscription-Paper and in the mean time you can have opportunity of seeing the Plan in my Shop.

I am,

SIR,

Your most obedient humble servant,

THOs. JOHNSTON
Praeses to the Stentmasters

In the event, the £450 subscribed by 333 persons was far from enough, and since the actual cost was £1,460 the Stentmasters fell further into debt from which they were not rescued by the sale of the old town clock in 1819 "for the price generally got for old iron."

The steeple had four parts. The ground floor was meant to serve as a town office but before long was being let out to shopkeepers. The first floor was the residence of the jailor in charge of prisoners who occupied cells on the third and fourth floors. These cells were equipped with heavy doors and grated windows. The bell which had rung out from the Old Steeple was fitted in the New in 1814 and was not pensioned off until 1897 when it was moved to the local museum.

As the 19th century advanced, the Stentmasters became less and less effective. They were severely criticised at the times of cholera outbreaks for the inadequate cleansing of the town, but the heavy burden of debt prevented them from taking any effective steps to bring improvements. By 1859 the Stentmasters could boast of no property, unless a debt of £1,900 could be thus considered. The interest on this debt was £100 and since their annual income was only £170, there remained a mere £70 for public use.

The second body which emerged in the 17th century to play a notable part in local affairs was the Feuars. The original feuars were fifteen proprietors who received titles to land in the High Street of Falkirk at the end of the 15th and beginning of the 16th centuries. They had the right of pasturage, feal and divot, and the quarrying of stones in the moor of Falkirk which in those days extended to some

55

150 acres to the South of the town. In general they were the most affluent of the burgesses. In 1807 while the new laird of Callendar, William Forbes, was proceeding with his policy of enclosing all open ground that could be used for agricultural purposes, the Feuars were prepared to renounce their rights and privileges on the town moor. In the Declaration of Commonty presented in the Court of Session, Forbes in return agreed to set aside ten acres of the moor as common property possessed by the Feuars. Twenty additional acres were to be enclosed by Forbes at his own expense, to be possessed in time as common property of the Feuars "to be managed and the profits applied in such manner as a majority of Feuars should deem for their and general good of the town."

"One acre of ground in the Callendar Riggs on which fairs are held" was to be "possessed as a market as a feu on payment of one penny Scots when asked." Finally Forbes surrendered to the Feuars "all customs capable of being exacted in the burgh" in the Horse-market and in the hay, corn, and butter markets in the High Street.

It would be misleading to leave the impression that these transactions amounted to much. In any year the customs dues netted £150 which taken along with the £50 in rents derived from the holdings on the moor, gave a grand total sum of £200. It is a remarkable thought that until 1859 the highest revenue raised by Stentmasters and Feuars for public service in Falkirk was £270.

In 1830 the Feuars set about the erection of a Corn Market. Up to that date grain was being sold in open stalls in the High Street and farmers and merchants were becoming impatient at the lack of covered accommodation, and threatening to take their produce elsewhere. The danger of a loss of revenue and the lowering of the status of the town led the Feuars to erect a small brick and wooden building against the North Wall of the Parish Church. This 1830 New Market was quite inadequate and in 1858 the Feuars determined to construct a proper Corn Exchange similar to those being built throughout Scotland. The site chosen was immediately to the north of the church in what was called Dr Corbet's garden. Dr John Corbet had his home at the north-east corner of the Lint Riggs, where the Newmarket Bar ultimately was sited. He is given the credit of having introduced vaccination against smallpox to the area, and his house was more usually called Vaccine House. Dr Corbet's garden which was renowned for the excellence of its flowers and shrubs ran along the north wall of the Parish Church. Though Corbet died in 1828 and his house until 1833 was used as a School for Young Ladies conducted by the Misses Whyte, and thereafter passed to Aitken's the Brewers, the plot of ground continued to be called Dr. Corbet's Garden. The Corn Exchange was duly built and the Feuars had to shoulder a debt of 'close on £1,600. Somewhere in the foundations of the Exchange was interred a glass bottle containing local newspapers, coins and a tuft of wool, a burial suggesting that the Feuars anticipated many years of successful operation before the relics were likely to be exhumed. Had they but known, the days of Feuars and Corn Exchange were to be limited because of the emergence of yet another body claiming to be the lawful custodian of Falkirk's civic interests.

In 1832, after the Great Reform Act, Falkirk was erected into a Parliamentary Burgh sharing an MP with Hamilton, Airdrie and Linlithgow. In this Parliamentary grouping, Grahamston and Bainsford were included in Falkirk. In the following year, the Municipal Reform Act prescribed that Falkirk should have a Town Council with a Provost and Magistrates. There was immediate hostility from Stentmasters and Feuars who, recognising a challenge to their authority, tried to frighten public opinion against the new body by stressing that having unpaid, unprofessional judges in the local court would threaten liberty and justice.

For twenty years the Town Council made little progress towards gaining effective power. Only substantial tenants and men of property had the vote in local elections and since most of these were represented in the Stentmasters or Feuars they were distinctly unsympathetic towards the radical change implied in the new form of local government. By the 1850s, however, there was a distinct change of mood. For one thing the emergence of the Falkirk Herald in 1846 gave a forum for educating public opinion. For another, there were very real and glaring shortcomings in the way the town was being managed. The climax came in 1859 when a Police Improvement Bill was introduced in Parliament to give real powers to the Town Council in the administration of public affairs. The evidence given at the Committee stage of this Bill in the House of Lords leaves a sorry picture of life in mid-19th century Falkirk.

"Although Falkirk is my own town, I do not know a dirtier in Scotland." The speaker was Mr John Gair, Procurator-Fiscal for the County of Stirling. "The supply of water is deficient. It is obtained from the old coal waste to the south of the town. There is some coal there still worked which tends to make the water a little dirty. It is an iron pipe that brings the water to the town. The water is good to drink but not for washing purposes." Several witnesses commented on the black particles of coal which became tangled in clothes. "The main pipe is in a bad state and is partially blocked. I estimate that 800 gallons an hour are wasted. Not above half a dozen private houses receive water. Most people have to get it from wells."

Offences at the wells of Falkirk had been in the public eye for some time. A bye-law of 1837 for instance declared that "no person may wash tripe, fish, potatoes, scullions or any other matter at the wells." Mr Gair went on to inform the Committee that "most houses have barrels to catch the rain water. There is nó public water supply to Bainsford and Grahamston. They have wells in their gardens which are perfectly sufficient in rainy seasons but are empty in time of drought." "I lived in Grahamston myself for some time," declared Mr Gair under cross-examination, "and was very troubled with the want of water. In summer the water was so offensive that I had to send a great distance for clean water. I had a well in my own garden and had to borrow water from a neighbour."

Mr Gair, Mr James Girdwood, surgeon, Mr Alex Black, land surveyor, and Rev. Lewis Hay Irving, Minister of the Free Church in Falkirk, all spoke of totally inadequate sanitary arrangements. "We have only one sewer. This is in the main street, and it gets choked up for want of water to flush it. There are very few water closets in the town, and the town therefore presents a most disgusting appearance especially the by-streets. Away from the causeway road there are nuisances before every door lying there for days together. The filth of Falkirk has become a byeword among all who have known it."

"The backhouses in Grahamston," complained Dr Girdwood, "are as filthy as possible. In getting down out of my gig even in the main street, I have to search for a spot where I may get down without soiling my feet."

Adding to the unpleasantness to sight and smell, were the presence of a number of slaughterhouses scattered among the dwellings. Though the day had passed when their owners could discharge blood and offal into the streets and sewers, they still did much to make an already evil-smelling town the more offensive. Well might the Falkirk deputation stress the danger to health. They were not slow to point out that the mortality rate of Falkirk was 87 per 1,000, while that of Edinburgh was only 60.

"The cholera was fatal in the ill-drained localities of the town such as Kerse Lane and the Howgate. Many houses," said Rev. L. H. Irving "are totally unfit for human habitation. The ground in the churchyard is black animal soil, the produce of decomposition, and it is from one to nine feet above adjoining houses. The drainage from the churchyard into a ditch which receives the refuse matter from the houses produces an abominable compound, and in the neighbourhood, typhoid fever often resulting fatally occurs."

Though the High Street of Falkirk was laid with causeway sets in 1851, it had few pavements. "There is no paving except what was

58

provided by private subscription twelve years ago. Some proprietors would not only not contribute to the paving but would not allow the improvements to take place before their houses."

Another cause of complaint was that street lighting was defective. The new gas lights provided in 1830 had soon been broken, and had not all been replaced. "There are a few lamps in the old burgh but in Grahamston and Bainsford none at all." This statement at the hearing was not strictly accurate for though there were none in Grahamston, Bainsford could boast a total of 12 lamps. The 44 lamps in the old part of the burgh were only lit in winter "and not then if there is moonlight. From April to September there is not a lamp lit from the one end of the town to the other. We are totally without light for six months whenever the almanac says there ought to be a moon."

"Apart from the inconvenience of the want of light," explained Mr Gair, "I know from my official position that it has led to a great number of street robberies and house breakings, and the Judges in Assize here have often remarked on the excess of such crimes in Falkirk." It was because of this undue amount of work provided by Falkirk that a Sheriff-Substitute was appointed for Falkirk to relieve Stirling in 1833 even if at the time Falkirk had no Court House.

One witness, however, was of the opinion that Grahamston and Bainsford were not really in need of street lighting because of the light provided from the blast furnace at Carron. To provide lighting in such circumstances would be a waste of public money "for near Carron a gas burner would be like the moon when the sun is shining." To him Mr Gair remarked drily that "it is a mistake that the Carron Iron Works light the street as it ought to be lit. It is too dark at night to find one's way about. When driving, the light is so glaring and flickering that it is rather a drawback than an assistance."

The upshot of all the evidence was the passing of the Bill which gave local government, vested in the Council, clear powers to bring improvements. Almost thankfully the Stentmasters repaired on 21st November, 1859 with their debt-laden books, documents and a statement of account, and there, handed over their powers and liabilities to the Town Council of Falkirk. The Feuars were, however, more obstinate. After all they had their New Corn Exchange and perhaps looked for a lucrative return. For forty years they held on tenaciously to their title to existence, although their powers were constantly being eroded.

In 1879 the Burgh Authority further reduced the importance of the Feuars by taking over the Corn Exchange and converting it into a Town Hall. This hall was to serve Falkirk until 1966, the Mecca of all

The Old Town Hall 1879-1966

forms of entertainment from public dancing to exhibitions, from drama and variety to choral concerts, from sports promotions to flower shows. Here too were held the other numerous activities of a healthy community—prize givings, evangelical missions, political meetings, polling counts and intimations of victories gained. Corn continued to be sold there until the end of the century.

Another monumental step towards a wholesome community was taken by the council in 1888 when after long public debate and the submissions of many schemes and counter-schemes, it was decided to obtain the water supply for the burgh from the Denny Hills. It was close on ten years before the first fresh, purified water flowed into a majority of homes in Falkirk, and indeed many families had to rely on pumps and wells for another generation.

Ten years before the hammer fell on the last auction of grain in the Town Hall, and before the new water began to flow, the Feuars agreed at last to bow off the public stage. Their property was handed over to the Burgh and so almost three hundred years after its baptism and after innumerable growing pains, Falkirk came to maturity with its first unified local government.

CHAPTER VII

THE CHURCH DISUNITED

Today when there are so many churches and shades of religious belief, it is almost surprising to look back on a time when Falkirk Parish Church was unchallenged as the only place of public worship in an area ten miles long and six miles wide. The supreme irony of the struggle which convulsed Scotland in the days of the Covenant is that it was fought to achieve church unity and conformity in religious observance yet in spite of the supposed victory of Presbyterianism in 1689, the Church was thereafter unable to prevent disunity and diversity. Perhaps it had taken a century of blood-letting to prove that in the quest for faith there are many roads.

From the earliest days after Presbyterianism became the Established Church, Anglicans were able to meet openly in defiance of the Kirk. Another deviant sect, the Cameronians, with its headquarters at Laurieston declared that it would stand apart until the Kirk renewed its mission to make all Britain Presbyterian.

The most important cause of disunity in the years after 1689 was however the question of lay patronage. In 1712 the Parliament in London re-established the principle that the local laird had the right to choose ministers even against the wishes of the congregation. "What difference does a piece of land make between man and man in the affairs of Christ's kingdom?" protested Ebenezer Erskine in 1733 when he broke with the Established Kirk. In February, 1739 with seven dissenting elders from Falkirk Parish Church forming the nucleus, there took place at Bonnybridge the first meeting of what was to become known as the Erskine Church. Within five years a large meeting house had been erected in Horsemarket Lane with Mr Henry Erskine, nephew of Ebenezer, as first minister. This primitive building was replaced in 1777 by a fine church in the Silver Row, with a manse and graveyard, which were to serve the Erskine congregation until 1905 when the present church at the corner of Hodge Street was occupied.

A further split came in 1747 when, after the Jacobite Rebellion, an oath of loyalty, the Burgher Oath, was demanded of every burgess in

61

Scottish towns. The wording of the Oath appeared to give recognition to lay patronage:

"Here I protest before God and your Lordships that I progress and allow with all my heart the true religion presently professed within this realm and authorised by the laws thereof. I shall abide thereat and defend the same to my life's end, renouncing Papistry."

Henry Erskine considered that his flock could take this oath without accepting lay patronage, but a large section of his congregation disagreed and broke away to form what became known as the Anti-Burgher Church. This sect had numerous meeting places, the first at

The Tattie Kirk

St. Crispin's Place. In 1806 the Tattie Kirk with its adjoining graveyard was erected. Some say that it was so called because it resembled a potato. Others suggest that it was built by money raised by the sale of potatoes. Perhaps it was built in a potato field, or as happened elsewhere in Scotland, its congregation may have been regaled between services with dishes of potatoes. In 1879 the church was deserted when the congregation moved to Graham's Road South Church.

In 1767 Falkirk produced yet another breakaway congregation, and again lay patronage was the cause. Six years before, Thomas Gillespie of Carnock near Dunfermline had set up a Presbytery of

Relief "for Christians oppressed in their church privileges." By 1766 there were 120 Relief Churches in Scotland, and the West Church with Mr Michael Boston as minister added to this number. Most of the present church dates from 1799 though a new frontage was added in 1883. Behind the church was the manse with a well-treed garden. A cemetery now derelict and overgrown lay to the west of the church.

In 1811 the Parish Church which had long been in a ruinous state was demolished only the tower remaining of the church that had so long served town and parish, a symbolic break with the past in keeping with its very changed status. For the process of secession and regrouping did not halt. In 1820 the Erskine and Anti-Burgher

Old Parish Church built 1811

Churches re-united in what was called the United Associate Congregation. They were joined in 1847 by the Relief Churches to form the United Presbyterian Church. Even more disruptive was the great breach which occurred in the Church of Scotland in 1843. As long as lay patronage endured there would be dissatisfaction with the Established Church. In that year Dr Thomas Chalmers led 470 ministers out of the General Assembly to form the Free Church. Dr Chalmers ironically had but recently preached in Falkirk Parish Church on the subject of church extension. Soon Free Churches were to spring up all over Scotland — church extension indeed! In Falkirk the first Free Church met in Cistern Lane but in 1844 moved to a new building in Garrison Place. It was from there that it transferred in 1896 to the present St. Andrew's Church, built on what had been part of the Parish Church Manse garden. In the 19th century, Lewis Hay Irving was minister and quite apart from his sustained efforts on behalf of his congregation was a leading figure in the agitation for better local government, a cleaner water supply, regular street cleansing, the provision of a Poor's House, a Ragged School where poor children might have some education, and a Savings Bank.

Another sizeable congregation outwith the Parish Church developed in the mid-19th century when the Roman Catholic population of the town began to rise. Immigrants flooded into Scotland from famine-torn Ireland. Highlanders ousted from their glens by the cruel Clearances sought work in the industrial belt. A chapel was built in Hope Street and served until 1963 when a considerable reconstruction on the same site took place.

The numbers and varieties of congregation outwith the Established Church continued to increase during the 19th century. In 1802 an Independent Congregational Church opened its doors in the building which now houses Young's Stores. Though this congregation disbanded in 1833 there were a number of other such congregations created at different times. In 1842 the movement called the Evangelical Union was strong in Falkirk. Its first congregation occupied the Congregational Church meeting place until its new church in Bank Street was ready in 1843. The Evangelical Unionists after many fluctuations in fortune joined a revived Congregational group in 1897 to form the congregation of St. James's.

The Baptist Church with a meeting place in Sword's Wynd had for a time a precarious existence, indeed in 1865 agreeing to disband. However its strength restored, it ultimately built a church in Callendar Riggs and later occupied its present building in Orchard Street.

A revived Evangelical Union congregation occupied the former Baptist meeting place in Sword's Wynd, moved to the Howgate and in 1893 to Meek's Road where the Meek's Road E.U. Church sought admission to the Church of Scotland. In 1896 when this congregation was restored to the Established Church, the name St. Modan's was given and it transferred to the Bank Street Church (subsequently The Picture House). At first St. Modan's was intended to be merely a Chapel of Ease for the Parish Church but so vigorously did its members accept all responsibilities and obligations that in 1915 it became a separate church, and its own very fine present building was occupied in that year.

Anglicans with their church in Kerse Lane, Methodists, Church of Christ, Salvation Army, Jehovah Witnesses, Plymouth Brethren and other minority denominations have all contributed to the complexity and variety of church-going in Falkirk.

If the all-encompassing nature of the Parish Church's control over individuals and families had been strikingly eroded since 1689, no less dramatic was the reduction of its territorial influence. In 1724 the lands of Eldrick, Easter and Wester Jaw, and Crostannie were added to Slamannan Parish. Castlecary and Seabegs were separated from Falkirk Parish in favour of Cumbernauld and Denny. At the same time an entirely new parish was created at Polmont incorporating Westquarter and Redding. As population increased and housing spread there was a further severance of new parishes — Camelon in 1853, Grahamston in 1875, Bonnybridge in 1878, Grangemouth in 1880, Blackbraes in 1890, Kerse in 1906, Laurieston in 1914 and St. Modan's in 1923.

By 1929 when the breach in the Presbyterian Church was healed by the reunion of Church of Scotland, United Presbyterian and United Free Churches, Falkirk Parish Church was only one church amid many, the only deference to its antiquity being the addition of the adjective "Old" to its name. Though at the time there were some harsh words spoken about this apparent arrogance, nowadays there are few to grudge Falkirk Old its name. It is after all the Mother Church of Falkirk, the parent church of all churches, Catholic as well as Protestant in the wide area that once made up its medieval parish.

Today, almost fifty years after the Union of 1929, there are those who say that Falkirk has too many churches, too many of them with too few members. In the last thirty years there has emerged a large element in the population with no connection with the church whatsoever. Many reasons are advanced for this drift from the Kirk. Some would argue that the church's middle of the road, middle class, middle aged image and its style of service with its passive congregation, its outdated hymns and its wordy sermons no longer appeal. The Kirk sits and talks when it should be acting. It is a materialist age, others will say, and things of the spirit are avoided or ignored. The seductions of the affluent society present more attractive alternatives to church attendance — the golf course, the television screen, the open road and the car at the door. Working mothers accept Sunday as a day in which to catch up with the chores and cook a specially attractive meal. Social and parental compulsion is now absent to a degree unimaginable in our grandfathers' day. Whatever the arguments, the fact is incontestable, the regular church-goers number only a small percentage of the total population of Falkirk, and with Sunday School and Bible Class attendance at their lowest point ever, there are no good reasons to expect a marked future change in the pattern of churchgoing.

Recently an experiment at reunion was undertaken at Grahamston, three churches enterprisingly uniting resources, manpower and finances so that they could be more effectively applied. Other congregations may well be driven to seek this course as economic and religious pressures mount with falling rolls. One thing is certain. It is unlikely that there will ever again be as great a measure of disunity in the Church in Falkirk as has occurred in the three hundred years since the days of the Covenant.

CHAPTER VIII

THE SECOND BATTLE OF FALKIRK

The news which came out of the West Highlands in August 1745 of a landing by Prince Charles Edward Stuart and the mustering of a Jacobite army must have struck alarm into the heart of any thoughtful Falkirk citizen. It was after all reasonable to suppose that if Prince Charles evaded the screen thrown up by Sir John Cope, he would strike at Edinburgh, and it did not require a profound geographical knowledge to recall that Falkirk lay on the main route to the capital. And as reports came in, each more ominous than the last, anxiety grew. Johnny Cope had missed the Prince. The highlanders were over the fords of Frew. They were past Stirling and encamped near Bannockburn.

It was therefore a distinct anticlimax when on 15th September the Jacobite force passed swiftly and uneventfully through the town and encamped "among some broom to the east of Callendar House." The Prince himself accompanied his army and spent the night "at my Lord Kilmarnock's at Callendar House beyond Falkirk; here he was informed that Gardner's Dragoons were encamped about five miles off at a little town called Linlithgow upon the road to Edinburgh. Upon this notice the Prince gave orders that there should be a detachment of eight hundred men chosen to strive to surprise the Dragoons in their camp."

"Having supped he retired to bed to prevent any intelligence being given of his design and went privately to the camp where he put himself at the head of the detachment and marched with a view to pass the river of Avon at the ford half a mile above the bridge and attacking the dragoons in the flank, but before he had marched above half way he got intelligence of the enemys having retired towards Edinburgh . . . so he took possession of the town of Linlithgow about six in the morning where the rest of the army joined him about noon."

Thus the Highland army marched towards the capital leaving behind a mercifully frugal crop of memories of its passage through Falkirk. In the following months townsfolk must have taken a detached interest in the course of the Rebellion. The capture of Edinburgh, the march on England, the retreat from Derby, must have appeared remote and

67

of little direct consequence. However early in January, 1746, the unpleasant fact emerged that Falkirk might not after all escape unscathed. On 3rd January the Prince began the siege of Stirling. A few miles away, on the north shore of the Forth, Jacobite reinforcements had reached Alloa, troops and artillery. The following day, 4th January, the worst was realised. Lord George Murray, chief military adviser to the Prince arrived at Falkirk with 1,100 men. This arrival caused Falkirk more than a little concern. It was not only that the conduct of the Highlanders was unpredictable and there were rumours of how Glasgow had been treated to add fuel to apprehension. There was also the unhappy fact that a very large government army assembled at Edinburgh, twelve battalions of infantry, two companies of dragoons and ten field guns, was on the move, and there was the very real danger that Falkirk might find itself caught between the two rival armies.

Henry Hawley, the government leader, was in a dilemma. He had word of large reinforcements en route for Scotland, yet he could not delay until they arrived in case the Castle of Stirling should fall. He had in any case a great contempt for the Highland soldier. "I do and always shall despise these rascals" he said, an opinion formed at Sheriffmuir in 1715 when he saw one cavalry charge disperse the Highland left wing. He therefore ordered his army forward. After a halfhearted skirmish at Linlithgow Bridge, Lord George withdrew his Highland units to the west of Falkirk leaving Hawley undisputed entry into the town on 16th January.

On that evening Hawley took up his headquarters at Callendar House, a dwelling which was no stranger to the Jacobite cause for in 1715 the Earl of Callendar had joined the Old Pretender and had lost his estates in consequence, and now his daughter, Ann Livingstone whose husband rode with the Prince, was the tenant. The fate of Callendar like the fate of the succession itself turned on the outcome of approaching events.

At 5 o'clock on the morning of Friday, 17th January, Hawley was astir, and after a hurried breakfast was on his way to the government camp to the west of the town. It lay westward of modern Hope Street and ran along the north side of the Old Stirling Road as far as present-day Dollar Park. Hawley was in confident mood. His plans were already laid. On 18th January, guides would lead his army over the fords of Carron and thus to Plean Moor where he would give battle to the rebels. Alas for Hawley! He was to learn that by marking time for twenty-four hours he had allowed the Jacobites to dictate the pattern of events.

The Jacobites were in good spirits. From the beginning of the year reinforcements had been arriving and the Prince could now count on the largest force which he had ever commanded, close on 9,000 men, fully twice as many as he had had for the invasion of England. At a conference held on Plean Moor on the morning of 17th January, the crucial decision was made. Lord George Murray's plan was that part of the Highland force under Lord John Drummond should allow itself to be seen at the Torwood, and that the Prince's flag should continue to fly on Plean Moor. While these diversions attracted the attention of Hawley's scouts, the main Highland force marching in two columns would make their way by sunken roads towards the fords of Carron and Bonny and thence on to Falkirk Moor.

The amount of Jacobite activity had not gone unremarked by Hawley's staff. "About eleven o'clock we got the alarm and in a very short space were all under arms and remained so a quarter of an hour. Then we found that it was a false alarm and we all turned in again and went to look out for dinner which was not easy to be found."

In Chambers' History of the Rebellion in Scotland is repeated a legend which has considerable acceptance locally, that one reason for Hawley's failure to take full precautions was his attraction to Ann Livingstone who acted as his hostess at Callendar House.

"On the morning of the battle such was his continued security that he obeyed an insiduous invitation from the Countess of Kilmarnock by retiring from the camp to breakfast with her at Callendar House, although quite aware of that lady's relationship to an insurgent chief, and even perhaps of her own notorious attachment to the cause of of Prince Charles. The ruse of the Countess was attended with complete success. She was a woman of splendid person and manners, and Hawley completely fascinated by her well-acted blandishments spent the whole of this important forenoon in her company without casting a thought upon his army."

Whether or not this is a just charge against Hawley, there is no doubt that he might have spent the morning more profitably. For the Highland march was getting underway across the Carron by the Steps of Dunipace, across the Bonny and in two columns two hundred paces apart swinging towards the highest ground on Falkirk Moor, Lord George making sure that the wind was directly behind the Highland army. During all this manoeuvre no challenge came from Hawley's regiments.

During the morning and early afternoon the Hanoverian army had "remained in their camp not altogether unapprehensive of an attack but yet strongly disposed like their commander to disbelieve that the Highlanders would venture upon so daring a measure." Hawley's force had been much heartened by the arrival of reinforcements. They could now count on twelve battalions of Regulars of the Line, 1,300 horsemen, militia from Edinburgh, Glasgow and Argyll, volunteers from Yorkshire, the Yorkshire Blues, in whose ranks was Blind Jack Metcalfe, later to make a name for himself as a road builder, and a Battalion of the Black Watch, close on 9,000 men in all. In addition there were field guns though all had grave doubts concerning the efficiency of the ever-drunk Captain Cunningham who was in charge of artillery.

"It was between one and two o'clock that several gentlemen, volunteer attendants on the camp coming in on the spur gave final and decisive intelligence of the enemy. They reported that they had seen the lines of Highland infantry evolve from behind the Tor Wood and cross the Carron by the Steps of Dunipace. The drums instantly beat to arms; an urgent message was despatched for Hawley."

"I never was used to these things but I was surprised to see in how little time their regular troops were formed (I think in less than half an hour) on their left of their camp in two lines with the Dragoons on their flanks; all fronting southe and just along the side of the high road leading to Stirling; the road in their front and Falkirk on their left."

Hawley "now came galloping up to his troops, his head uncovered and other marks about his person betraying the haste with which he had left the hospitable table of Lady Kilmarnock."

"We all thought that there we were to wait for the Enemy who was plainly in view coming along the hills from the South-West. Mr Hawley it seems had another notion for no sooner was the army formed than he marched them straight up a steep hill which lies to the south-west of Falkirk in two Columns in order I suppose to gain a large moor which they say is on top of the hill and which may be so for me and I believe for his Excellency too; for neither of us saw it at least before the action."

Today when television makes us eye witnesses of conflicts in different parts of the world, we are all too familiar with the agony of civilians caught in the path of the oncoming tide of war. At Falkirk on that late January day, for on the old calendar the 17th January is the equivalent of our 28th January, there were many harrowing scenes of refugees fleeing in search of safety.

"The people dwelling between the present positions of the two armies in the dreadful expectation of being speedily involved in the horrors of battle were at this moment in a state of great alarm . . . They might be seen hurrying to and fro across the country equally uncertain where danger was to be avoided or safety to be sought. Some were attempting to transport articles of property . . . and others seemed only anxious to save their children and aged relations."

"A number of citizens of Falkirk stationed themselves upon the fortified bartizan of the steeple . . . uniting their gratification of curiosity with a desire for safety . . . One of the children who survived until recently (1827) used to tell that in this short and dismal journey she well remembered crossing the lines of the Royal army near the entrance to Bantaskine House where it stretched across the road . . . As the men gave way to allow a passage for the children a hare started up near the place and ran through the lines; upon which the soldiers raised a loud view-hollo and one more ready-witted than the rest exclaimed, "Halloo the Duke of Perth's mother!" it being a general belief that that zealous Catholic lady was a witch and therefore able to assume the disguise of a hare . . . for the purpose of spying the English army. The soldier's exclamation was received with shouts of laughter."

Laughter was, however, to be short-lived as the grim business of war was set underway. Led by the dragoons, the army climbed up Maggie Wood's Loan "swearing as they went along with all their proverbial fury and venting the most ferocious threats against the men they were about to encounter." In the dip just beyond the summit of the loan the cannon stuck. Local tradition says that Cunningham, unable to get horses, employed local carters who, perhaps unwilling to get any closer to the Highland army, ran their guns into the mud, cut the traces and galloped their horses back to Falkirk. It was an event of significance for Hawley had no use of his cannon in the battle that was to follow. In that the Highland cannon stuck in the Carron it was to be an engagement of small arms, naked steel and courage.

The route up which the royal army climbed in an effort to reach the summit before the Jacobites is steep and broken, and worse, as the troops struggled upwards, the storm which had been threatening, broke, and wind and rain lashed their faces. The sky was overcast and it was prematurely dark. And so drenched, short of breath, apprehensive, critical of their general, the government troops came over the last crest into view of the Jacobite force. Here was ground which Hawley was seeing for the first time, the unfittest possible for regular troops. Gone was the false assurance of an hour or so ago. There were few who did not question what lay ahead when the two armies clashed.

In the Battle diagram (page 72) the centre of the field is marked by the monument which now occupies the site. To the south the ground rises to the 400 foot contour and then falls towards the Glen Burn. The south side of this hill was very marshy and Lord George was quick to position his right flank so that it had the protection of the swamp. The most conspicuous feature of the area is a ravine which runs northwards widening as it reaches the flatter ground. Though the

71

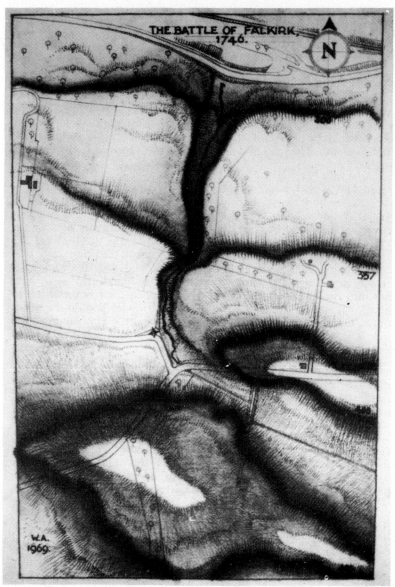

Battle Diagram

Union Canal was not built until 1820 it has been added so that the extent of the battlefield may be more clearly gauged.

In the race for the summit, the Highlanders led by Lord George were successful. When he reached the crest he waited until the remaining regiments came up, and then the whole Highland force swung in a great arc until they stood due north and south.

The various contemporary accounts of the battle reveal considerable variation in the matter of how the Highland force lined up. The majority opinion was that the front line from right to left was made up of three MacDonald Regiments led by Keppoch (400) Clanranald (350) and Glengarry (900). Then came the Farquharsons (150), Mackenzies (200), Mackintoshes (300), MacPhersons (400), Frasers (500), Camerons (900) and Stewarts (300). In the Second Line, the Atholl Brigade (900) was on the right. Then came two Battalions commanded by Lord Ogilvie (900). Further to the left were Lord Lewis Gordon (800) and Lord John Drummond (400) who came up with his Irish piquets after the battle had started. The Third Line was made up chiefly of horsemen. On the right stood Lord Elcho and Lord Balmerino with 220 horsemen. In the centre was the Marquis d'Eguiles with French and Irish piquets (300). On the left were placed Lords Pitsligo and Kilmarnock with some 220 horses.

"The Prince with his own guards and Fitz James's horse from France posted himself immediately behind the centre of the foot at about twenty yards distance that he might have a necessary and commanding view of the whole."

The Front Line of 4,500 men, the Second of 3,000 men and the Third of 740 men gave the Jacobites a total strength of just over 8,000 men. One remarkable omission which was to have serious repercussions in the engagement was that no one was placed in charge of the left wing of the Highland army.

The Hanoverian army which struggled into position drew itself up with its dragoons on its left flank. These three regiments were under the command of Ligonier who was suffering from pleurisy and was to die two days later from the exposure to wind and rain on Falkirk Moor. His dragoons and those commanded by Hamilton had been supplied with new horses which were not battle trained. Only Cobham's detachment had seasoned mounts.

The infantry came up to form the centre and right wing of the government force. They inclined north-east because of the ravine. Each unit numbered some 660 men and as was the custom in those days took the name of its commander. The front line was therefore made up of Wolfe's, Cholmondley's, Pulteney's, the Royals, Price's and Ligonier's. Behind stood the Second Line of Blakeney's, Munro's, Fleming's, Barrel's, and Battereau's with Howard's in reserve. The

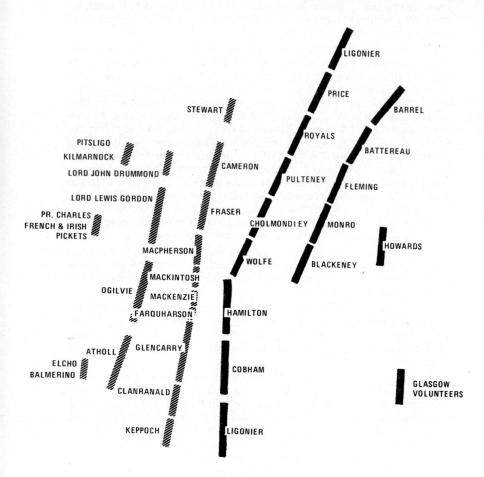

ARGYLL MILITIA

LIGONIER

PRICE

BARREL

STEWART

ROYALS

BATTEREAU

PITSLIGO
KILMARNOCK
LORD JOHN DRUMMOND

CAMERON

PULTENEY

FLEMING

LORD LEWIS GORDON

FRASER

PR. CHARLES
FRENCH & IRISH
PICKETS

CHOLMONDIEY

MONRO

HOWARDS

MACPHERSON

WOLFE

BLACKENEY

MACKINTOSH

OGILVIE

MACKENZIE

FARQUHARSON

HAMILTON

ATHOLL

GLENCARRY

ELCHO
BALMERINO

CLANRANALD

COBHAM

GLASGOW
VOLUNTEERS

KEPPOCH

LIGONIER

BATTLE ORDER

74

Glasgow Militia which "being newly levied was not allowed to have a place either in the First or Second Line" stood by itself near some cottages behind the left of the dragoons. The Argyll militia were given the task of safeguarding the route to the government camp and were stationed at the foot of the hill.

The two armies had roughly the same number of men although in his battle reports Hawley estimated that he had 2,000 men more than his adversaries.

Thus the two armies stood in position, miserable in the driving rain, each man thinking those thoughts peculiar to the moments before battle. When would the signal come? What did the next hour hold in store? Ligonier was not however idle. He had sent out patrols in the hope of finding a way of outflanking the enemy. But Lord George had chosen his ground well. After floundering into and out of the clinging morass to the south of the Highland position, the scouts were back confirming what Ligonier had suspected from the start. The only way in which to engage the enemy was by that straight but hazardous approach in face of the Highland army. He therefore called on his dragoons to form line, and two hundred paces apart the left wing of the government force glowered towards the blurred outline that was the Jacobite right, the only sounds in that strange lull, the champing of horses, the moaning of the wind and the staccato patter of rain on saddle leather and on targe.

Lord George Murray had decided to fight on foot, a decision which he was later to regret. He had taken off his wig, pushed his bonnet firmly down on his forehead and with broadsword and target was striding back and forth exhorting the Macdonald clansmen not to fire until he gave the order, and above all not to break rank in pursuit should the enemy turn tail.

"The infantry of the King's army not being completely formed . . . when General Hawley sent an order to Colonel Ligonier who commanded the cavalry to attack the rebels." Ligonier looking round vainly for infantry to come up in support protested that the order was "the height of rashness," but was told shortly to be about his business.

So Hawley launched the royal attack. It was just before four o'clock. Ligonier, Cobham and Hamilton gingerly edged forward towards the waiting Highland army in the hope of drawing their fire prematurely, so that they could charge before they had time to reload. But the clansmen had been well instructed by Lord George. Grim of face they stood their ground, half-crouching, their muskets menacingly undischarged.

There was to be no easy victory. Ligonier accepted the inevitable. The order was given and at a full trot the horsemen headed for the

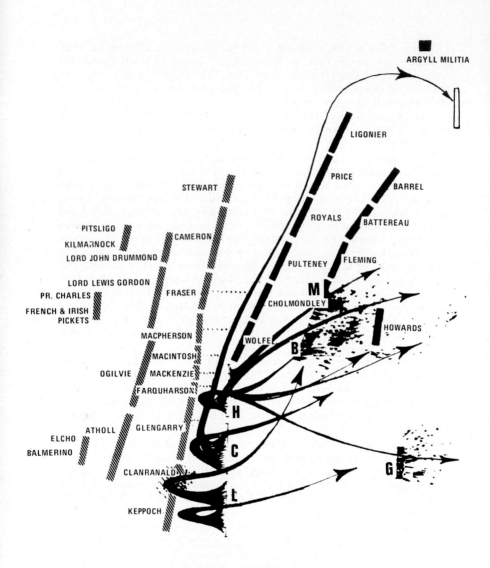

ARGYLL MILITIA

LIGONIER

PRICE

BARREL

STEWART

ROYALS

BATTEREAU

PITSLIGO

KILMARNOCK

CAMERON

LORD JOHN DRUMMOND

LORD LEWIS GORDON

PULTENEY

FLEMING

PR. CHARLES

FRASER

M

FRENCH & IRISH PICKETS

CHOLMONDLEY

HOWARDS

MACPHERSON

WOLFE

B

MACINTOSH

OGILVIE

MACKENZIE

FARQUHARSON

H

ATHOLL

GLENGARRY

ELCHO

C

BALMERINO

G

CLANRANALD

L

KEPPOCH

BATTLE - PHASE 1

76

enemy line. As they closed within fifty yards the spurs dug deep and a quavering cheer rang out as the trot became a full gallop. Nerve-shatteringly silent, the Highlanders stood musket to shoulder, and from Lord George still no order.

Thirty yards . . . twenty yards . . . even the battle hardened Jacobite veterans began to fidget. Was he leaving it too late? Ten yards — and suddenly Murray's arm was raised.

The volley was devastating. In an instant eighty dragoons fell dead blown from their saddles by the closeness of the discharge. Horses stumbled coughing from blood-flecked mouths. Others fell silently, killed on the spot, slithering grotesquely forward on the rain-soaked ground.

Perhaps it was the raw horses for the first time meeting gunfire. Perhaps it was the irresolution of the horsemen. Perhaps it was the almost awesome fear of the Highlander that had grown in Hawley's ranks. Whatever the reason, dragoons sheered away in all directions from the Highland line.

At one point only did they have a measure of success. The grim courage and inspiring leadership of Lieutenant-Colonel Whitney encouraged some of Ligonier's men to hold on to break through Clanranald's first rank. Whitney himself was shot dead as he reached

Lionel Edward's Painting   'The Battle of Falkirk'

77

the line and so did not live to witness that remarkable and terrifying method used by the Highlanders to deal with such an emergency.

For as the horses overran them, the Jacobites fell down and with their dirks thrust upwards slitting along the bellies of the horses as they passed over them. It was a moment of horror, horses screaming, blood spurting from gaping wounds, horsemen being dragged from their saddles and dirked, howls of agony and terror and hopeless defiance from those unhorsed and ringed by merciless foemen. The survivors turned and fled.

In the wild panic of flight Hamilton's dragoons rode over the Glasgow Regiment "among whom I was" writes Corse, "& would then have given my life for a shilling," while Ligonier's men swept away the left wing of the foot before they had the opportunity to be in action. For Cobham's Regiment there was an even more spectacular exit from the battlefield. They galloped down the line of the ravine between the two armies like moving targets at a fair inviting the attention of every Highland marksman along the whole front rank. Many dragoons paid the supreme penalty for this folly.

As the Hanoverian left wing collapsed in confusion, nothing could restrain the impetuosity of the Highlanders with the scent of victory in their nostrils. Though Keppoch's men stood firm, Clanranald's and Glengarry's regiments, forgetful of all Lord George's pre-battle entreaties, threw down their firelocks, drew their claymores and with a full-throated roar leapt forward in pursuit. They did not charge alone. The Regiments along the line of the ravine who had fired at Cobham's dragoons now stood with their firearms discharged and unable to meet an assault by the royal foot. Highlanders did not use cartridges. Their guns were loaded with the use of powder horns, an operation futile in heavy rain. Undeterred they threw down the useless weapons, drew their swords and in a solid mass hurled themselves forward towards the redcoats.

At Falkirk the royal foot-soldiers had had much to daunt them. There had been the suddenness of the alarm, the exhausting race to the moor up steep, broken slopes, the discomfort of the unrelenting rain carried by gale force winds beating upon their faces. There was the gnawing doubt that their general did not know his job. There was concern lest their muskets misfire at the crucial moment and there would be no time for the reload. Above all there was now the awesome spectacle of this ungovernable human tide bearing down upon them. As a man they turned and fled.

Wolfe's, Cholmondley's, Pulteney's, the Royals, all turned tail. With them went the second line all except Barrel's. At the foot of the hill the Argyll Militia took their cue from the regiments of the line

78

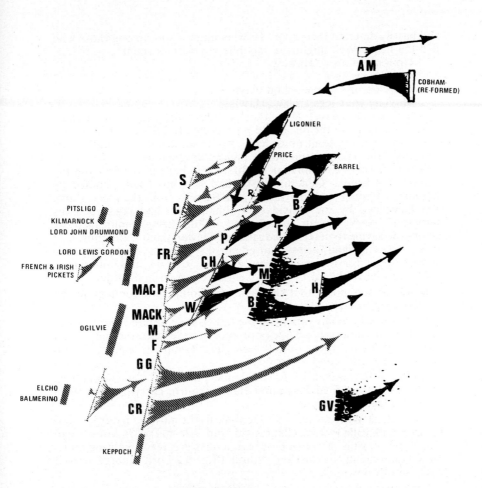

AM

COBHAM-
(RE-FORMED)

LIGONIER

PRICE

BARREL

S

PITSLIGO
KILMARNOCK
LORD JOHN DRUMMOND

C

R

B

LORD LEWIS GORDON

FRENCH & IRISH
PICKETS

FR

P

F

CH

M

MAC P

W

B

H

MACK
M
F

OGILVIE

G G

ELCHO
BALMERINO

CR

GV

KEPPOCH

BATTLE–PHASE 2

and hastily deserted their post. Hawley himself was among those who fled the field. Well might the Jacobite rhymesters chant:

"Up and rin awa', Hawley,
Up and rin awa';
Tak care or Charlie's guid claymore
May gie your legs a claw, Hawley."

It had been too easy! Were they perhaps being drawn into a trap? Surely regiments of the line could be expected to offer more resistance than this. The cry went up to halt. While some uncontrollable units continued the wild pursuit, others paused uncertainly.

It was at that moment that the first real challenge came from the Hanoverian army. General Huske had kept his head. Joined by Ligonier's Foot, Price's Battalion and Barrel's from the second line, and heartened by the arrival of Cobham who had regrouped his survivors, Huske began to advance uphill, firing simultaneously across the ravine to deter the advance of Stewarts and Camerons.

As the Highland army paused in its charge, they offered a perfect target for the government troops. Caught in a murderous flank fire, the Highland Left and Centre collapsed in disorder.

It was at this point that the lack of a competent commander on the left wing was felt.

"Had there been any officer on the left to have ordered two or three battalions from the second line or reserve to have faced the enemy that outflanked them, they would have had complete victory." So considered Lord George Murray.

Suddenly all was confusion, Highlanders fell back, some not halting until they had reached Plean and Bannockburn, carrying with them news of a Jacobite defeat.

As the Left Wing retired, the Jacobite Right moved forward. Lord George had called after Clanranald and Glengarry, bidding them reform but in vain. His two best regiments were lost as fighting units. Now summoning forward the Atholl Brigade, Lord George moved purposefully downhill.

"At this moment the field of battle presented a spectacle seldom seen in war . . . Part of the King's army, much the greater part was flying to the eastward and part of the rebel army was flying to the westward. Not one regiment of the second line of the rebels remained in place; for the Atholl brigade being left almost alone on the right marched up to the front line and joined Lord George Murray where he stood with the Macdonalds of Keppoch. Between this body of men on the right of the first line and the Camerons and Stewarts on the left (who had retreated from the fire of the troops across the ravine) there was a considerable space altogether void and empty, those men excepted who had returned from the chase and were straggling about in great disorder and confusion with nothing in their hands but their swords."

A moment of crisis arose to heighten the uncertainty of the outcome. Cobham's Dragoons had crossed the ravine and were galloping uphill threatening to overrun the area where the Prince was stationed. Seeing the presence of some Irish piquets and Highlanders of the reserve Cobham turned back. Thereafter Huske and the three foot regiments covered by Cobham fell back on Maggie Wood's Loan where he was able to drag out three of the deserted guns, for which feat his men were later to be kissed by their Brigadier and each given ten guineas. As Hawley himself testified in his report:

"Had not the brave General Huske with two battalions, Ligonier's and Barrel's put a stop to the Highland pursuit, I do not know where it might have ended."

A hurried debate was taking place among the Highland leaders. Some were for halting the advance. At a rough estimate Lord George considered that he had scarcely 700 men. It was at this point that he bemoaned the lack of a pair of bagpipes.

"Our vast loss was that not a pair o' pipes could be gott. The pipers whenever the battle begins give their pipes to their boys who take care of themselves and the Pipers are commonly as good men as any and charge with the rest."

It is doubtful, however, if even the sound of the pipes would have drawn the clansmen from the plundering that was taking place, nevertheless he was determined that there would be no return to Plean. He was "absolutely for marching into the town for he said if the enemy had the least time they might line the houses and clean their guns," and make the town a fortress. He rounded off his speech with Count Mercy's expression at the Battle of Parma that he would either lie in the town or in paradise. "His Royal Highness . . . approved of the resolution of attempting the town and was advised himself to stay at some house on the face of the hill till Lord George Murray sent him word of the success."

Lord Kilmarnock who knew the district well was despatched to reconnoitre the position. He was soon back with the news that most of Hawley's men were streaming eastward towards Linlithgow. Thereupon the command was given to enter the town.

For the citizens of Falkirk the afternoon had been one of high drama and nervous concern at the outcome. Those who climbed the Steeple of Falkirk in order to view the battlefield were surprised how quickly the firing was over, according to some reports just ten minutes. Then came the alarming sight of dragoons wildly fleeing the field, thundering through the town. And then, the harrowing spectacle of riderless horses staggering down the Cow Wynd, many so weak with loss of

Falkirk Steeple from an Old Print

blood that they were scarcely able to walk while others trailed behind them their entrails. Then came the foot soldiers making no pretence of being any other than an army in abject flight. Among them was Hawley who gave orders to set fire to the tents, and local tradition has it that in frustration he broke his sword against the Mercat Cross before retreating to Linlithgow "leaving behind him seven pieces of cannon with a great quantity of provisions, ammunition and baggage."

Falkirk was soon occupied. Locheil entered from the West End, Lord George Murray by Bantaskine Port (now Roberts Wynd) and Lord John Drummond by the Cow Wynd. As Lord John reached the junction with the High Street there was a sharp skirmish with some Hanoverian troops some of whom were killed and Lord John wounded.

Finally when all precautions were taken the Prince was sent for and lodged in the Grand Lodging, the house of Mrs Graham, the widow of a surgeon who had been a keen Jacobite. The room where the Prince slept the night, it is said in a press-bed, is that room immediately over the doorway of what is now Watson's shoe shop opposite the Steeple.

"His Royal Highness's first care early next morning was to cause bury the dead as well those of the enemy as our own people." To those assigned this unpleasant task the early morning light revealed the ghoulish work that the hours of darkness had concealed. For

82

PRINCE·CHARLIE'S·
LODGING·
AT·FALKIRK·
·DEMOLISHED·1899·

during the night robbers had stripped the dead of all that they possessed and they lay, it seemed unnaturally white in the cold dawn looking "nothing so much as like a flock of sheep."

The dead were placed in pits dug on the battlefield, in the strip of trees between Lochgreen and Slamannan Roads, in the Ravine, in the copse now at Dumyat Drive, and by the High Station. Highlanders were to be recognised by the bannock that many carried under their left arm pit. Of Hawley's men there was no doubt. The claymore left its own distinctive mark.

There are grim stories of that morning, burial parties burying wounded as well as dead, one protesting soldier being told:

"Och just you be going in quiet like just to please the Prince!" At another point a passer-by records the sight of a Highlander pulling feverishly at the shoes of a dead English officer, straddling him the better to tug, calling at each effort, "Braw brogues, braw brogues!"

It was some time after the battle before all the casualties were finally laid to rest. Some weeks later one unfortunate woman crossing a stream, saw the face of a dead Highlander grinning up at her through the water. She lost her reason as a result of this incident.

There is some conflict of opinion as to the number of casualties. According to Elcho, Hawley lost 30 Officers and between 500 and 600 other ranks. Home reported 16 Officers and 300-400 other ranks killed, and Kirkconnel 400-500. Johnstone stated 600. Hawley himself put his losses at 12 Officers and 280 other ranks but there is no doubt that he under-estimated. Murray counted the number of government prisoners as 300 including the hangmen engaged by Hawley to execute the rebels, but Chevalier Johnstone says that many more were captured on the following day in surrounding villages to the total of 700. Jacobite losses were 7 Officers and 43 men dead. Between 60 and 70 were wounded and only one man was taken prisoner, the unfortunate Macdonald of Tiendrish who captured a horse which loyally decided to rejoin its regiment with the short-lived new owner clinging to its neck. He was hanged a few weeks later at Carlisle.

One tragic aftermath of the battle was the accidental shooting of Young Glengarry in the High Street of Falkirk:

"A private soldier of the Clanranald regiment had obtained a musket as part of his spoil upon the field of battle; finding it loaded he was engaged in his lodgings in extracting the shot; the window was open and nearly opposite there was a group of officers standing in the street. The man extracted the ball and then fired off the piece to clear it in the most expeditious manner of the powder, but unfortunately it had been double loaded and the remaining ball pierced the body of Young Glengarry who was one of the group of bystanders. He soon after died in the arms of his clansmen begging with his last breath that the man of whose innocence he was satisfied might not suffer; but nothing could restrain the indignation of his friends who immediately seized the unhappy perpetrator and loudly demanded life for life. Clanranald would gladly have protected his clansman but certain that any attempt he could make to that effect would only embroil his family in a feud with that of Glengarry and in the first place cause that regiment to quit the Prince's service, he was reluctantly obliged to assent to their demand. The man was immediately taken to the side of a park wall near the town and pierced with a volley of bullets. His own father fired a shot into his body from his desire to make his death as instantaneous as possible."

"The Prince who had most occasion to regret this accident as it endangered the attachment of a valuable regiment exerted himself by showing the most respectful attentions to the deceased to console the clan for their loss. He caused the grave of Graham which had never before been disturbed to be opened for the reception of the youthful soldier as the only part of the churchyard of Falkirk which was worthy to be honoured with his corpse . . ."

It was later revealed that the grave of Scotland's hero of 1298 was not after all disturbed, the grave diggers preparing a grave a few feet to the south of the de Graeme tomb. In 1870 when the grave was opened to erect the present monument, only one body was found in it and that of a burial much earlier than 1746.

The other Jacobite memorial in the Churchyard is the Munro Tomb. This monument was raised in 1750 to mark the burial place of two brothers, Sir Robert and Obsdale Munro, a surgeon who loyally followed his soldier brother as a non-combatant. Munro's son tells the tale:

"My father after being deserted was attacked by six of Locheil's regiment and for some time defended himself with his half-pike. Two of the six he killed. A seventh coming up fired a pistol into my father's groin upon which falling the Highlander with his sword gave him two strokes, one over the eyes, the other in the mouth, which instantly ended a brave man. The same Highlander fired another pistol into my uncle's breast and with the sword terribly slashed him."

The parish church of Falkirk was used to quarter prisoners. A letter sent by one prisoner to his family in Glasgow gives some idea of conditions:

"This is to let you know that I am alive and in pretty good health considering my ill bedding. I'll warrant you there are more than three hundred of us lying upon straw in the kirk but there are many more in the Tolbooth of the town and in the cellars of Callendar that do not

85

The Monro Tomb

fare so well. The Highlanders are not so cruel as we thought them. When the Minister of Fala reads the Bible and we sing psalms, the Guards take off their bonnets. But I am sorry to tell you that the English redcoats go to the other end of the kirk and all the time of our worship are cursing and swearing and damning us as Presbyterian Dissenters."

Hawley withdrew to Linlithgow where on the night of the battle he wrote the following despatch to his superior, the Duke of Cumberland: "My heart is broke. I don't say we are quite beat today. But our left is beat and their left is beat. We had enough to beat them for we had 2,000 men more than they. But such scandalous cowardice I never saw before; the whole second line of foot ran away without firing a shot."

He had changed his tune within a day:

"Saturday, January 18th: I am to report that I have given a severe check to the Highlanders. The evening being excessively raining I thought it proper to march the troops to Linlithgow and put them under cover there, otherwise we should have continued in our camp at Falkirk being masters of the field. There was too the danger that the rebels might push between us and Edinburgh. We lost 300 men but it is much worse for the Highlanders . . ."

A day later Hawley was in Edinburgh where he ordered fourteen deserters to be hanged and thirty two soldiers to be shot for cowardice. There were four hangings in the first day in the Grassmarket. Many soldiers were publicly whipped. Five officers were court-martialled. Cunningham the gunner committed suicide. Perhaps the only man who was glad of Hawley's failure was Johnny Cope who, it is said, won £10,000 which he bet on Hawley's being beaten.

Within a little over a week the Jacobite forces had withdrawn from Falkirk to Stirling leaving certain citizens of the town with niggling fears of what reprisals the government might take against suspected Jacobites. They need not have worried. No action was taken against Mrs Graham in whose house the Prince spent the night after the battle. Indeed local tradition has it that the Duke of Cumberland in his procession towards Stirling actually spent the night in the same room and in the same bed that his cousin had occupied being sure he said, "that it would not only be the most comfortable but also the best provisioned." No reprisal was had against one hundred other citizens "who gladly housed the rebels," or against the carters who ran Hawley's cannon into the mud, though the Kirk Session did complain of those "who went to the field of battle and pulled off horse shoes and the shoeing of cartwheels which was not their own." One young Jacobite captured after Culloden was John Auld of Falkirk aged 14, who pleaded that his father had forced him to march with the Highlanders. Lord Kilmarnock's declaration at his trial that "he had been unable to raise one man for the cause of the Stuarts in Falkirk" was therefore perhaps correct. For the Lord himself there was to be no clemency. In August, 1746 he was beheaded on Tower Hill.

We are left to contemplate the "ifs" of the Battle of Falkirk. If Hawley had had no preconceived ideas of how the Highlanders might be beaten; if he had covered the crossings of Carron and Bonny; if he had had a competent captain of artillery; if he had not dined so well at Callendar House; if he had reconnoitred the area round Falkirk so that his men could have fought on suitable ground; if he had delayed the advance of cavalry until Ligonier had infantry in support; if the rain had held off another half hour; then Falkirk might well have been the Culloden of the Jacobite cause.

We may of course argue the Jacobite case. If a thousand men had not been left besieging Stirling Castle; if the Highland Right Wing regiments had stood as commanded; if there had been a Left-Wing

Commander; if Murray had had a horse or a set of bagpipes, then a more complete victory might have been gained. But no matter how complete, it could merely have postponed the inevitable. Skirmishes in the rain might still be won by the extraordinary methods and unbridled ferocity of the Highland soldier, but a skirmish does not win a campaign, any more than do dreams of a Crown gain a Kingdom.

Battle of Falkirk 1746 Monument

CHAPTER IX

FALKIRK TRYST

It was the Tryst which first put Falkirk on the national map. Earlier, Crieff had been the great stockyard of Scotland, but as more and more land in that area was fenced off for cultivation the amount of grazing for the large herds and flocks was reduced to a point where an alternative site had to be found. Hawick and Stirling made their claims. Hawick's more southerly position placed it closer to the rich urban markets of North-East England, but Highland drovers objected to the extra miles along which their beasts inevitably lost condition. Stirling made a stronger challenge. All roads north and south funnelled through this town. Its merchants and shopkeepers, tradesmen and hostelry owners were quick to appreciate the rich annual pickings that would come their way should the Tryst be located on their doorstep. Close to Stirling were the growing centres of population in Edinburgh and Glasgow, and the road south to Newcastle was not impossibly long.

It was Falkirk, however, that won most favour. It had all the advantages offered by Stirling. It had in addition wide acres of rough pasture, and it was this consideration that resulted in the Tryst being established at Falkirk.

The Tryst until the 1770s was held on Redding Moor. When, however, enclosure progressed in that district, the Tryst was moved to the Roughcastle-Seabegs area, which never was popular. For one thing there were many old coal and iron workings which claimed frequent victims among the livestock. For another, there was the formidable obstacle presented by the Forth-Clyde Canal which cut its way straight through the middle of the Tryst ground. After 1785 the Tryst was transferred to Stenhousemuir where it made its permanent home.

The second Tuesdays of August, September and October were the Trysting days. It became the custom for the August sale to deal exclusively with black cattle, and the other meetings with cattle and sheep. Horses were sold at all Trysts. In the heyday of the Tryst in the mid-19th century as many as 50,000 cattle, 40,000 sheep and

5,000 horses were on sale. Down the drove roads they came from the Western Isles and the West Highlands, from the Central Highlands and East Scotland north of the Tay, from Fife and Lothian, from Ayrshire and the West.

Along the drove roads lay many dangers, the would-be rustler, the lame beast, the swollen stream, the impassable marsh, the sea or ferry passage. Vigilant and hardy, the drovers made a fetish of always arriving on time. Sleeping out in all weathers, sustained by a rough diet of oatmeal and whisky, this sturdy breed earned well the one shilling a day received in pay.

The Tryst ground in the mid-19th century was a cauldron of activity: Milling cattle, the bleating of sheep, the voices of auctioneers hammering down lots, the melee of dialects, Highland, Lowland, Gaelic and the broad Geordie tongue of Tyneside, the clatter of carts about their business of collecting manure, fish lassies crying their wares, hot soup stalls, ale and food tents, entertainers, acrobats, sideshows, swings, shifty pickpockets, sightseers. Noise, excitement, hard drinking continued long after dark, spilling into the many hostelries and ale houses throughout the district.

Buying and selling was by letters of credit accepted by branches of the leading banks set up in tents at strategic points on the Tryst ground. No money changed hands, only the cancellation of this or that figure on a letter of credit and the sealing of a deal with a handclasp and a dram. For the seller, the transaction concluded, there remained the prospect of the homeward journey laden with household or farming equipment hard to come by in the more remote regions. For the buyer there was the start of his worries. Where were the most lucrative markets? Which route through the Borders and Cheviots would be safest and quickest? What dangers lay along the many long Scots miles separating him from the profits which awaited the first herds to arrive on Tyneside?

As the 19th century advanced the importance of the Tryst began to wane. New breeds of animals were being produced, bred for better beef and unable to make the long journey as readily on the hoof. New macadamised roads were much harder on the hooves of animals than the old drove tracks. Indeed for a time it was necessary to shoe cattle as well as horses, and smithies for this purpose sprang up along the many trails to Stenhousemuir. On some stretches of new road tolls had to be paid, raising thereby the final price of animals. The enclosure movement was spreading rapidly so that it became increasingly difficult to obtain free grazing by the wayside. Farmers who recognised the commercial significance of providing pasture for passing herds charged dearly for the privilege of grazing, thus making the price of cattle from remote areas even less competitive. Better rotations of crops provided winter fodder and ruled out the need to have the huge autumn slaughter of beasts that had been necessary since the start of animal husbandry.

It was, however, the railway that dealt the fatal blow. With the provision of a nation-wide network of railway lines, it was no longer necessary to drive cattle for long distances on the hoof. They could be carried speedily and in prime condition to their final destination by rail. Buyers, therefore, began to seek out cattle as they required them. Local cattle markets began to spring up throughout the land and the Tryst declined.

By the turn of the 20th century the great days were over. Horses continued to be sold into the 1920s but the Tryst had become more or less a funfair, though at a time when pleasures were more simple and less numerous, it was still one of the important occasions in the local calendar.

Today the Tryst weekend still attracts its annual pilgrimage to Stenhousemuir. For some it is a short journey lightened by the excitement that comes of novelty. For others there is the more uncertain quest, the hope of recapturing the pleasures of some years long past. Some go more resignedly, bowing to the pressures of families and friends, while others, the slaves of custom, head for the Tryst because they have always gone. Whatever the motive those who hie to the broad acres of Stenhousemuir are keeping alive a tradition which stretches backwards across two centuries. In other parts of Scotland, similar local fairs robbed of their original purpose are declining and some have indeed died. Is this to be the ultimate fate of Falkirk Tryst? Whatever its future it has been a remarkable institution.

CHAPTER X

THE ECONOMIC REVOLUTION

(i) Before 1759

Falkirk before 1759 gave no hint of the remarkable economic revolution which lay ahead. Still a small market town serving fewer than 4,000 souls, it stood in an essentially agricultural area looking out over a wide expanse of unenclosed field, marsh and moorland, broken on three sides by occasional villages dotted over the carseland between Carron, Avon and Forth, and southwards over the rising, undulating country towards Redding and Slamannan Moors. Farming was the main occupation, and there were few families who did not have some contact with the land either as full-time or seasonal labourers. Wages were by modern standards ludicrously low. A ploughman earned between £2 12/- and £5 per year together with bed and board. Female servants could expect under 30/- annually with their keep and "Sunday claithis and shoon." Casual workers had between 4d. and 10d. a day.

Much of the land was "poor, wet and spungy," and the yield was low. It is significant that in times of scarcity, which were all too frequent, English and foreign grain sold in Falkirk markets, and this in an age when the region had sufficient resources properly husbanded to have supported itself. The traditional Scottish lowland system of farming in narrow, curved rigs prevailed. March stones served to separate one holding from the next. The frequent redivision of rigs offered little incentive to the improver. Land thus remained undrained, unlimed, under-productive, for what farmer was willing to labour only to see the benefits pass to someone else at the next reallocation of rigs?

There was little industry. From 1723 Aitken's Brewery occupied the site east of Hope Street where it was to stand until 1970. There was a cottage industry in spinning, weaving and bleaching linen, the modern Bleachfield behind the Town House echoing in its name a once-familiar local trade. There were, too, the inevitable tinsmiths, coppersmiths, blacksmiths, the hatters, tanners, saddlers, tailors, carpenters, masons, bakers and shoemakers, but none of these trades accounted for a large labour force. In the region outside the town there were the colliers, some of them until 1775 bought and sold with their shallow pits, and largely a race apart, for they rarely married outside their own society.

In 1759, then, all unaware of its future, Falkirk stood at the threshold of great changes which were to transform completely its appearance and the tempo of its way of life.

(ii) 1759-1820

The sixty years after 1759 brought important, though socially catastrophic, changes to the farming community. The impetus to progress came from the Enclosure Movement. With evidence before them of the commercial benefits of Enclosure in England and elsewhere in Scotland, the more influential landowners and tenants pressed for reform of the age-old field system. It was not however until the 1780s when William Forbes bought Callendar Estate that the impulse towards enclosure accelerated. Within twenty years a transformation had taken place in the appearance of the countryside around the town. Everywhere there were straightened rigs, and the familiar pattern of fence, hedgerow and dyke was replacing the open fields which for a thousand years had been the accepted face of farming. Moorland and marshland were not to escape the march of progress. Forbes was in the van of a reclamation programme. Farmers were rented a few acres which had to be limed for two years, on the second of which grass was to be laid down. Land overrun by heath and broom was to be ploughed five times and then sown with grass provided by the laird.

Security of tenure allowed go-ahead farmers to adopt the new techniques spreading throughout Britain. Drainage, liming and marling went on apace. New breeds of cattle and sheep were introduced, and experiments in rotations of crop took place. The standard rotation in the Falkirk area in 1800 consisted "in general of six parts: First the ground is fallowed; secondly it is sown with wheat; thirdly with beans and pease; fourthly with barley; fifthly it produces a crop of grass for hay, the seeds of which had been sown the preceding year with the barley; and sixthly it is sown with oats." The annual Trysts provided the region with a plentiful supply of cheap manure.

One other notable feature of the late 18th century was the start of afforestation. Callendar Estate was again in the forefront of progress in a movement soon copied by other local lairds. So, an area once famous for its woods, but remarkable for its lack of trees since the 17th century, began to regain the aesthetic, climatic and economic advantages of well-wooded surroundings.

Falkirk's destiny was not however to lie in agriculture. In the late 1750s the fate of the locality became inextricably linked with that of the nation. Britain in those years stood at the crossroads in her history. Across the seas an Empire was waiting to be won. At home, industry was poised on the brink of a fantastic revolution that was to sweep the country to pre-eminence in manufacture and banking. Without more iron neither destiny would be fulfilled. Even had the Seven Years' War not cut off supplies of high grade Swedish ore, there would have been need for more ironworks using native ore.

It was such considerations that in 1760 brought a red glow in the sky above Carron, and ushered in a new age for nation and town. It needed Dr John Roebuck's vision, Samuel Garbett's business acumen, and William Cadell's knowledge of the Forth Valley to single out Carron as the location of their new ironworks. The site had much to commend it. In the days before the hot blast furnace and before there was an economical steam engine to work machinery, water power was essential to operate the leather bellows of the cold blast furnace.

There was at Carron ready access to local supplies of iron ore. Those from Bo'ness were considered to be superior to any on the Forth. Coal was necessary for coking and collieries at Bo'ness, Kinnaird, Carronhall and Shieldhill were close at hand.

Carron stood, moreover, near the sea. It would not require a deal of effort to dig a canal to Carronshore and the Forth. The sea lanes of the world would then be open to carry produce across the earth and to bring back vital raw materials such as ore and timber. It was not enough in 1759 to have only coke for smelting. Pig iron thus obtained though adequate for the hard and brittle cast iron from which were fashioned pans, grates, farm implements and even cannon was not capable of withstanding the hammering encountered by wrought iron. Charcoal was needed for the smelting of this higher grade pig iron. Since Scottish timber had all but disappeared there was advantage in being close to a port through which Scandinavian and Baltic timber could be imported.

"It will be a fine thing" declared Samuel Garbett, "to get a large fall of water very near to Bo'ness coal and ironstone and likewise near the sea." Carron had other assets. Fireclay and limestone were amply obtainable locally.

Last minute opposition came from Cadell who had revived earlier proposals that the works be established near his family estates at Prestonpans. His partners, however, disagreed and the Carron Company was founded in 1759 and the first furnace came into blast on 26th December, 1760.

One disadvantage of Falkirk as an iron producing centre was the lack of skilled labour. Garbett was unwilling to use Scottish workmen and imported his labour force from England. As a result the Ironworks were soon to be called locally "the English Foundry." There were numerous unpleasant incidents between Scots and English. "The narrow-hearted in Falkirk scruple not to say that our coming into the country will be as dangerous as a French invasion."

The earliest days of Carron were fraught with uncertainty. Part of the trouble lay in frequent managerial disputes, and in the activities of Samuel Gascoigne, Garbett's son-in-law, who contrived over the years to squeeze out each of the original partners from control. The failure of the early models of the Carronade brought the Company near to ruin in the 1770s. However, an original milling process saved the Carronade and the Company. From that moment the firm's motto "Esto Perpetua" had good hopes of fulfilment. The Carronade was used by both British and French navies during the French Revolutionary and Napoleonic Wars. Its contribution to our island history is perhaps too often ignored, but there is little doubt that it brought fame and fortune to Carron and Falkirk.

As Carron consolidated and extended its activities, its effect on the area became more pronounced. Villages to house workers sprang up at Bainsford, Grahamston, and Stenhousemuir. When there proved not enough water from the Carron, a dam, 30 acres in extent, was built, and from time to time heightened. The meandering Carron was straightened although as a matter of interest its old course may still be traced from studying existing parish boundaries which once followed the Carron and have never been altered. A canal from the works to Carronshore was cut, a distance of half a mile.

When it became clear that there was not enough ironstone to be had from Bo'ness, digging commenced at Brightons and Maddiston with a consequent extension of housing in these areas. Coal, too, was in short supply and new pits were developed at Callendar, Bo'ness, Brightons and Carronshore. The Carron Company continued its policy of employing English in preference to Scottish workers by importing men from Shropshire to work in the pits. "The Scots are undeserving men who will not work." "The English are remarkably sober and commendable and live in decent fashion." In fairness to the Scots it should be remembered that Scottish miners were in bondage whereas from the start the English received better wages.

It soon became plain that the greedy furnaces at Carron would not be satisfied from the tired reserves of surface coal in the area, and Roebuck proposed a revolutionary development. He would sink a deep pit. The site chosen was at Kinneil, but a prerequisite was an efficient pump. James Watt was engaged and his momentous separate

95

condenser engine was the result. Unfortunately, bad workmanship at Carron brought failure and placed Roebuck close to ruin from which he rescued himself only by selling the patent rights of Watt's invention to Matthew Boulton, the Birmingham manufacturer. As it happened the same design of engine constructed with more precision at Birmingham offered Man a wonderful source of power that was to transform his way of life, one of the great milestones in the human story, which might have borne the trade-mark "Made in Falkirk."

Among the many famous visitors to Carron was Robert Burns who had the distinction in 1786 of being denied entry to the works by a zealous porter. Burns left a wry testimonial of his visit in the following lines:

"We cam na here to view your warks
In hopes to be mair wise,
But only, lest we gang to Hell
It may be nae surprise.
But when we tirl'd at your door
Your porter dought na bear us
Sae may, should we to Hell's yetts come
Your billie Satan sair us."

An event as important to Falkirk as the founding of Carron was the opening of the Forth-Clyde Canal. It had first been suggested in the reign of Charles II and surveys had been made in 1722 and 1761, but it was not until 1767 that the work got underway. John Smeaton was the architect. By 1775 the canal had reached the outskirts of Glasgow where it had to be suspended through lack of funds. In 1784 money raised from the sale of forfeited Jacobite estates allowed the project to be completed. By 1790 ocean to ocean travel was possible, and Falkirk found itself within cheap and easy distance of the expanding heartland of Scottish industry on Clydeside.

One of the most dramatic early incidents in the history of the canal came in 1802 when William Symington launched the first steamship ever built, (into its waters). The Charlotte Dundas, its engines manufactured at Carron, was constructed at Grangemouth. Large crowds gathered to watch history being made and great cheers greeted the stately passage of the tiny steamer as, smoke reeking from its long funnel, it surged westward along the canal. The Canal Company, however, fearing that the wake would endanger the sides of their new canal refused to let it proceed further. The ship thereafter lay in one of the passing bays and was gradually demolished by action of weather and curio hunters. Symington died a poor man. Not so two of the sightseers who swarmed over the stranded vessel in its first days of quarantine. Robert Fulton and Henry Bell carried away ideas which they built into their own ships soon to ply on the Great

96

Lakes and rivers of America and on the Clyde, bringing them personal fortune and the world a more efficient mode of transport.

The second Canal to serve Falkirk was begun in 1818 and ran from Port Hopetoun in Edinburgh to Port Downie in Falkirk. It was completed in 1822 by the construction of a system of locks stepping

Union Canal at King's Bridge, Camelon

down to join the Forth-Clyde Canal west of Lock 16. In the last mile of this waterway was built the first communications tunnel in Scotland. Irish labour was chiefly used and the strawhuts of the navigators were a source of wonderment in the locality.

By 1820 the scene was set — Carron, Canals, expanding industry, new farming, mines, the Tryst—Falkirk had come a long way from the days of being a small market town.

(iii) 1820-1880

In spite of industrial advance, agriculture continued to employ the greater portion of the population for another three generations. They were unhappy years for those on the land. As the Industrial Revolution began to concentrate population in towns and cities in Central Scotland, the more astute farmers were not slow to appreciate the financial rewards that progressive farming would bring. They were therefore ruthless in their bid to outstrip their poorer rivals, who, lacking the capital for improvement or for the fencing which the law required around their fields, had no alternative but to sell out to their richer neighbours and to join the class of landless labourers. In Falkirk as elsewhere in Scotland the worst effects of the Enclosure Movement were felt in the 1830s. For the first time since the Middle Ages there was a sizeable body of landworkers possessing no land and relying for their livelihood solely on the sale of their labour, a commodity of uncertain value in an age of massive unemployment, when the full and awesome panoply of the law was used by the ruling classes to resist any organised attempts by workers to win improved conditions.

Although social distress was acute, much improvement in farming was evident. New equipment such as the swing plough, new harrows, seed drills and threshing machinery became commonplace. Drainage did much to reduce the extent of marsh land and to lighten the soil. Better rotations of crops eliminated the wasteful fallow. In the fields around Falkirk in the 1830s experiments in potato cultivation were surprisingly successful in view of the disdain felt hitherto for this crop by Scottish farmers. The number and quality of animals also increased.

Towards the end of the period under review, farmers suffered in common with others throughout the country. The forging of the railroad across the American prairies in the 1870s brought Europe within easy reach of cheap American grain which rapidly undersold native corn. In consequence farmers were forced to alter their traditional methods. The mixed farm, part arable, part pastoral, became standard in the Falkirk area. Mixed farming required a smaller labour force and workers were dismissed. Farmers, ruined by the cost of adaptation, sold out and larger farm units were the result. The hard times were reflected at the feeing fairs held at Callendar Riggs and the Steeple in the late 1870s and 1880s when at the end of the day, there was the regular spectacle of a considerable group of unengaged workers standing anxiously amid their families and pathetic bundles, forlornly contemplating an uncertain future.

Industrial advance was constant during these sixty years. In 1828 the invention of the Hot Blast Furnace allowed smelters to use blackband ore with three times the yield. Carron, though slow to change its smelting process, ultimately came into line. By the 1870s competition from English ironworks, particularly at Middlesborough, led to the decision to rebuild the works. New furnaces capable of utilising spent gases were built increasing production by 20%. The Carron Company also continued its quest for locally produced coal. The reports of the conditions in the mines in the 1840s are particularly distressing in the light of the apparently sincere belief of the Company that its colliers were well treated. When the fault is not recognised there is little hope of improvement. Thus until 1842 the 23 children under 13 and the 43 young people of 13-18 worked in the most trying circumstances.

"I work on long days 15-16 hours." "I draw in harness and sister hangs on and pushes behind. The work is gui sair and we often get knocked doon as the cart goes doon the brae." A cart held five hundredweight of coal. "My present employment is to bucket water and lift to a level face. The work is constant and most wearying as the place I lift is low not four feet high." "My earnings are 10d. a day and it costs me 7d.-10d. weekly for oil and cotton." There were many accidents and no compensation for injury. So in Falkirk as elsewhere, industrial advance and company prosperity were bought at a heavy personal and social price.

There are frequent references in early times of hostility to the growth of Trade Unions, workers being sent to the Tolbooth in Stirling to "think better of their ways," summary dismissals and other forms of persecution of those suspected of organising combinations of workers. The most dramatic involvement of Falkirk in the early history of Trade Unionism and Radicalism came in 1820 when government agents sought to stampede malcontents into the open by spreading the rumour that the workers of Falkirk had risen and captured the arsenal at Carron Ironworks and were holding out in the hope of support. Thus misled, a large mob set off from Glasgow blundering into a carefully laid ambush of government troops on Bonnymuir. The ringleaders were arrested and executed at Stirling.

The success of Carron proved the touchspring for a release of industrial energy. Go-ahead workers and acute businessmen combined to plan rival foundries. The first of these, the Falkirk Iron Company was founded in 1819 and soon other foundries emerged, Union in 1854, Abbots in 1856, Burnbank in 1860, Grahamston in 1868, Larbert in 1870 and Camelon in 1872.

The wide range of goods which poured out of these foundries makes interesting reading: shot and shell, stoves, inkstands, umbrella stands, garden seats, verandahs, statues, mirror frames, weighing machines, fly wheels, window frames, spits, bedsteads, staircases, printing machinery, pipes, hoes, railings, girdles, sugar presses, money chests, and a hundred other items of industrial and domestic use.

Another industry associated with Carron was the Nailworks at Camelon, at one time employing 250 men and boys. A less desirable feature of this enterprise was its use of pauper children who were on occasion cruelly treated by their overseers. Nailmaking was a lucrative employment, one man and three boys earning as much as 28/- a week. How much of this wage was profitably spent is open to

Carron Company

doubt, for the nailers of Camelon were notorious for drunkenness in a district not celebrated for its sobriety.

Another development prompted by the Carron Company was the founding of a shipping line with the monopoly of carrying the firm's produce. Jobs were thus created for sailors, ship builders, ship repair workers and dockers at the Carron Wharf.

The Canal, too, attracted industry. In the period after 1820 there was a spate of building along its length. Chemical works, muslin, cotton and linen manufactories, tanneries, brick and tile works, brewing, saw mills, woodyards, rope works, corn mills, and a distillery came into operation.

Even more important ultimately in the industrial future of Falkirk than the canals was the coming of the railroad. In 1838 a multitude from the whole district gathered on the Union Canal to the east of the town to await their first view of the new marvel of the times, a locomotive drawing its line of coal trucks from Stanrig by Airdrie along the Slamannan Railway to the wharfs constructed at its terminus at Causewayend. As the chugging monster hoved into view a ragged cheer greeted the start of a new age. Within four years the North British Company had routed its Edinburgh to Glasgow line through the High Station. The first train had thirty carriages, each of which cost £400. In each carriage there were three "apartments" with six passengers in each apartment. The seats had cushions and "stuffed arms" and were "like easy chairs." There was glass in the doors and glazed panels on each side.

Of great interest was the tunnel immediately to the east of the High Station. It was opened for three nights before the first train came through. The entry fee on the first night was 1/-, on the second 6d. and on the third 3d. During the construction diggers came across the remains of soldiers killed in the Battle of 1746.

In 1846 another significant line, the Stirlingshire Midland, came through Falkirk from Polmont to Stirling over the Skew Bridge and the Embankment to Grahamston Station and a swing bridge over the Canal at Camelon. Though providing an additional valuable communications link, this railroad had the effect of adding to the difficulties of north-south travel within the town, already divided by the Forth-Clyde Canal.

The years before 1880 then brought a new face to Falkirk. They inspired, too, a new vitality as industry expanded and diversified. By 1880 because of catastrophic changes in farming, the balance had at last swung and for the first time, industry could claim to have superseded agriculture as the chief employer of labour in the Falkirk area. The gulf between rich and poor widened and the high proportion of young women in poorly-paid domestic service is a pointer to the new social pattern. Many families lived just above, and not a few below, the poverty line, and the Poor's House was an ever-present shadow in too many lives. There were, however, sufficient workers able, often at the cost of great sacrifice, to save regularly to encourage the emergence of a Savings Bank, Friendly Societies and Building Societies. Nevertheless for all but a few fortunate individuals, the great wealth created in Falkirk did little to improve the quality of life, the lot of most workers being low wages, inadequate housing and the constant anxiety of what was to befall at the next trade recession or the next bout of sickness.

(iv) 1880-1939

Quite the most significant feature of this period was the surrender of much arable land for housebuilding. The reaper and binder were to be seen in fields where once the sickle and scythe had won the harvest. Insecticides and chemical fertilisers made slow progress. Afforestation proceeded wherever land was available and the landlord was in favour. Otherwise the pattern of agricultural change at Falkirk was no different from elsewhere in the central belt of Scotland.

The industrial scene did, however, show continuing development. In 1867 the Caledonian Railway Company had gained control of the Forth-Clyde Canal. Its chief rival, the North British Company therefore began to build branch lines throughout the area in order to divert traffic away from the canal. A further strategy was the

Bainsford Bridge

provision of sidings for any company that wanted the railway to run into their works. Thus began a most significant trend. Up to 1880 the main location of industry had been along the canal. With the promise of railway service to their works' door, firms began to move away from the canal on to the railroad. Over a number of decades the process continued, until at length the only industries left on the canal between Grahamston and Camelon were those relying on it for water supply. By 1966 through traffic on the canal had ceased.

Railway rivalry had a further impact on industrial Falkirk. The Caledonian Railway was all too aware that its only port on the Forth was Grangemouth and was at pains to develop port facilities. In 1882 and again in 1906 Grangemouth had extensive improvements. A new dock, timber basins, independence from the River Carron, an artificial entrance with locks, all provided a port of 58 acres far superior to its rival at Bo'ness. A marshalling yard was laid out and ship building and repair yards set up. The proximity of such a valuable shipping terminus was not lost to industrialists seeking to locate industry at Falkirk. Better modern transport, the cheap bicycle and ultimately the motor car and bus allowed many Falkirk workers to have employment in Grangemouth so that, though divided by civic and local rivalries, the two communities were drawn together by economic bonds. Thus the S.C.W.S. Soapworks, opened in 1897, the I.C.I. Dyeworks in 1919 and the Scottish Oils in 1923, refining Shale oil from West Lothian, were to be important for Falkirk as well as Grangemouth.

In Falkirk itself there were not monumental changes in the pattern of industry apart from its relocation. Galvanisation of metals and the opening of a Hosiery in 1924 were the only developments of note. Indeed the Depression of the 1930s brought hard years of recession when six foundries closed their doors.

(v) 1939-75

After 1939 agriculture was of little significance in the total economy of the town. The mechanisation of farming reduced the work force even further, and it is an interesting comment on progress that the yield from this much reduced acreage by reason of new fertilisers, improved seeds, insecticides, selective weedkillers, and new farming methods is greater by far than for the best year of the 19th century with a much wider acreage available for cropping.

Industrial progress has, however, been most impressive during these years. In 1943 an Aluminium Rolling Mill went into operation at Bainsford. There was little to commend the site apart from good communications and a supply of highly qualified metal workers. Ingots had to be brought long distances, and the rolled products were far from the chief markets which were in England. However, Falkirk was all too willing to benefit from the wartime strategy of dispersing vital industries.

In the years since the war the cheap, undeveloped, level, tidewater land at Grangemouth attracted British Petroleum. Arab nationalism and the dangers of the seizure of capital equipment such as occurred at Abadan in 1951 convinced the company that the best policy was to build native refineries supplied by fleets of tankers. The small Scottish Oils plant was bought over and Grangemouth Refinery and its attendant Hydro-Carbon industries sprang up.

This decision had far-reaching effects on dock installations at Grangemouth, and these in turn made the whole area more attractive for investment. New industrial estates grew up round Falkirk. Today on the eve of regionalisation, Falkirk is the home of many industries— ironworks (all castings for Carron ceased to smelt after 1963), aluminium sheet rolling, chemicals, bookbinding, pre-cast concrete, fireclay and brickworks, timberyards and sawmills, tar distillers, engineering and coachworks. With North Sea Oil all but in the pipe line, the future for the whole Falkirk-Grangemouth complex is full of promise, though it is unlikely that any other two hundred years will experience the dimensions of the economic revolution that has befallen Falkirk since 1759.

CHAPTER XI

A WALK THROUGH THE TOWN

To walk along Callendar Road from the Skew Bridge towards Falkirk is to march with history. Here is one of our nation's most ancient highways. Few there are who have earned renown or notoriety in our country's past who have not travelled its length. The medieval monarchs with their retinues passing between Linlithgow and Stirling, William Wallace, Edward I, Edward II, the Scottish rebels convening at Falkirk before the Battle of Sauchieburn, John Knox and the Protestant Lords, their faces towards Edinburgh and victory against the French and Catholic forces of Marie de Guise, the tragic Mary, Queen of Scots, the pedantic James VI, the reckless Charles I, the stolid Cromwell, the dashing Montrose, the romantic Young Pretender, the ghoulish body snatchers, the staid Victoria, the host of great men of letters, of science, of industry, of politics, of the church, traders and travellers, bearers of good and evil tidings, unwitting carriers of disease—all have used this road, an exciting assortment of the great and the humble, of the dramatic and the commonplace who have helped shape the destiny of Falkirk and the Scottish nation.

Until this century Callendar Road was a tree lined track running between fields to the north and Callendar policies to the south. Enough has been written about Callendar, its house and families, and of the Roman Wall in other chapters. On the right of the road the first feature of significance is the Pikes where, last century, cricket matches were played, the earliest recorded being in 1836. Later, Falkirk Football Club considered building its stadium on this site. More recently the sporting connection has been maintained by the use of the Pikes as school playing fields. Nearer Falkirk stood the Hedges, a passing place on the otherwise single track tramway to Laurieston, opened in 1905. It was at this point that Falkirk Technical School was erected in 1932.

The Meadows to the west of the school have had a chequered career as farmstead, town rubbish tip and public park. Across its acres wandered the Meadow Burn or as it was more often called, the East

Callendar Road and East Bridge Street

Burn. This water rose in Callendar Estate and flowed under the East Bridge on its way to Ladysmill. The Burn until recently marked the Burgh boundary of Falkirk.

Opposite Graeme High School, old Callendar Road turned into the Callendar policies and made its way through the trees until it made a sharp descent to the East Bridge, climbing thereafter up East Bridge Street to the High Street. The line of this old road may still be seen close to the High Flats which have become a feature of modern Falkirk since their construction in 1962. Not until 1829 was the section of road which runs from the present Bus Station to Bell's Meadow opened. Its development sentenced the East Burn to going underground and East Bridge Street to a secondary role.

At the single span East Bridge stood Marion's Well, taking its name from a nun, Marion Livingstone who was said to have used the waters for medicinal purposes. Later the trough of the well was moved to Callendar Road at its junction with Corporation Street.

The area running southwards from Callendar Road towards the East Bridge was for many centuries the playground of Falkirk. Here men and boys played their skittles, the Goose and other games of chance. Here Volunteers trained during the Napoleonic Wars. Here, too, more sombre rites were performed, for the gallows of Falkirk were sited at this place and public hangings are on record, a grim gibbet brooding over the scene where youngsters and adults played. This area was called the Claydens, surely a more desirable name than Corporation Street!

105

To the south of Callendar Road, roughly on the site occupied by Crawford's Garage, stood the Gas Works which served Falkirk until 1846 when they were moved to Bainsford. Opposite, on the north side of the road, stood Belmont House, withdrawn behind high walls and guarded by a lodge which still stands. The members of the Smith family who were its owners, were hyper-sensitive about their relationship with Madeline Smith, the central figure in a celebrated Victorian murder trial. Later, when the house was demolished contractors made full use of the fine sand on which it was erected, and a large sand pit was dug. Outwith the grounds of Belmont and opposite the present Labour Exchange was discovered a valuable cache of Roman coins, now in the Museum of Antiquities in Edinburgh.

High Street from East End

The entry into Callendar Riggs at the beginning of this century squeezed between the first building in the High Street and a long line of billboards stretching along Callendar Road. It was a rough, unsurfaced track, climbing sharply. Today, some idea of the slope may be had by examining the height of ground still left at the side of Doak's Dancing Academy. Until the 1920s this elevation carried over to the Silver Row. Enormous quantities of soil had to be removed to make the present flat Callendar Riggs. Where now the car park, shops and bus station are located there were once the grounds of a stately home called Rose Park. When it was demolished, the open space created was visited twice yearly by show people with their stalls and roundabouts. On occasion feeing of farm workers also took place at this spot. Children from the Catholic School in Silver Row used this area as a playground, a practice frowned on by the local constabulary.

To the north of Callendar Riggs ran the Randygate, the modern Kerse Lane, once notorious for its bad housing, its poor drainage and its frequent fevers. After 1878 a long wall enclosed the orchard which is recalled in street names such as Orchard Street, Garden Street and Garden Terrace. The Ragged School for children whose parents could not afford regular schooling moved from East Bridge Street to Kerse Lane in 1859, the building ultimately serving as a model lodging house. Close by, on the opposite side of the road, a public slaughter house was at last provided in 1873 after vigorous pressure to remove all butcher yards from the town.

Manor Street and Bank Street from Kerse Lane 1925

So the road dropped away from Falkirk under the railway bridge built for the Stirlingshire Midland Line in 1846, down past Ladysmill and thus to the low countryside leading to Grangemouth where the Ice Rink, Falkirk Technical College and the Middlefield Industrial Estate have been built.

Few parts of Falkirk have changed as completely as the area to the west of Callendar Riggs. Many concerns have occupied premises on the north side of the High Street between Callendar Riggs and Alexander's Stores only to fall victim to the formidable onslaught of competition and progress. Alexander's has endured since 1835 and has lived on to extend not only its Falkirk shop between High Street and Manor Street, but also its business empire to other towns. But the Red Lion Inn where so many important functions were held last century with its very extensive stables stretching behind and the Cosy Corner Tavern with its gay conviviality have all passed into oblivion.

Silver Row

The area to the east of the Red Lion Inn in the 17th century was called Rashiehill, and was much favoured by the well-to-do. The best known of its residents in those far off days was Murehead of Rashiehill whose elaborate tomb may still be seen in that part of the Parish Churchyard behind St. Andrew's Church. Beyond the Red Lion Inn, a lane well known to all Falkirk folk whose memories range back over the few years since the opening of the Callendar Shopping Centre linked the High Street with Callendar Riggs. Once called Kerse Pend it was renamed Horsemarket Lane after the establishment of horse auctions in Callendar Riggs in 1801. Cutting across this lane was the Silver Row which climbed steeply from the High Street and fell more gently towards Manor Street. The most notable building in Silver Row was the first Erskine (East U.P.) Church. After the removal of the congregation in 1905 to their new church at Hodge Street, the church building housed a variety of activities. Rooms in the front of the church were used by mission groups whilst the main body of the kirk became first the Electric Theatre showing silent films and later the Roxy Theatre on whose stage many famous stars of vaudeville performed. Close to the Roxy stood the Catholic School, while at the corner with Manor Street was the Masonic Arms, a tavern which claimed association with Burns when he visited the town in 1786.

Construction of New Shopping Centre

109

There is nothing as final as a bulldozer. Previous ages have left behind them foundations and relics of the past beneath new construction. Today, however, nothing remains when constructors clear a site, and this was the fate of this whole area in 1963.

For many years the Steeple of Falkirk has been the civic centre of the town. Here, long before the days of newsprint, public proclamations were delivered. Here were held the two weekly markets and the four annual fairs permitted under the burgh charter. Round the Mercat Cross, the site of which is marked by a circle of causeway sets, was enacted many a lively scene, stallholders, fish lassies, fruit vendors, all calling their wares, buyers and sellers of cattle, sheep, pigs and poultry, earnestly seeking the best deal, and countrymen displaying vegetables, eggs and all manner of other produce to the jostling crowds.

Here offenders against the rigid laws of their day faced public censure—the victim in the stocks, head defiantly raised or shame-

Cross Well at the Steeple

facedly lowered; the scolding wife placed in the branks, its iron tongue temporarily at least giving her husband respite from her slanging; the wrongdoer writhing under the strokes of the cat-of-nine-tails at a public flogging; the faltering criminal goaded his last few despairing steps to the gallows. The last public hanging in Falkirk took place at this spot in 1826. In gayer mood, the Steeple was the rallying point for Hogmanay revellers ushering in the New Year with song, good cheer and a dram.

The Cross Well below the Steeple dates only from 1817 but it is certainly a replica of the original bequeathed to the town in 1681 by the Earl of Callendar. The figure of the lion atop this fountain is incorporated in the Town Crest.

Last century a most surprising addition was made to the environs of the Steeple, a statue of the Duke of Wellington whose presence must have caused many a visitor, and indeed many a Falkirk Bairn,

Lightning Damage to Steeple, 1927

111

to wonder why the victor of Waterloo should have been accorded such an honoured place in the centre of a Scottish Burgh. The reason was no more complicated than that Provost Adam liked the appearance of this particular piece of sculpture when he visited an exhibition of the work of Robert Forrest, the Lanark sculptor. The price £130 seemed reasonable. A public subscription soon raised the money. So the Duke moved into residence—but only until 1905 when the inexorable march of progress forced his retreat to Newmarket Street where he now stands sentinel. Of the merits of this statue little comment is required beyond that of a Frenchman who, after regarding it long and earnestly and from many angles, exclaimed "Now Waterloo is avenged."

Over all these changes and activity, trivial and important, commonplace and momentous, gay and sombre, the Steeple of Falkirk has presided for more than four hundred years. In June, 1927, a bolt of lightning struck the steeple. Thirty or forty feet of the tower were hurled to the ground. It was providential that at the time of the accident a torrential rainstorm had cleared the streets. As it was, a horse yoked to a lorry owned by Barr & Co., Aerated Water Manufacturers, was directly below the falling masonry and was killed instantly.

Immediate steps were taken to restore the Steeple which today is classed as an Ancient Monument by the Department of the Environment and thus enjoys a measure of protection from all but another bolt from the blue.

To the east of the Steeple and on the North side of the High Street is Wooer Street so called from the old Scots name for a weaver, though there is no evidence that weavers worked here after 1800 when the name first appears in town records. It seems to have suffered from a most unsavoury reputation last century, and respectable citizens were careful to give it a wide berth after dark. It was notorious for its second-hand clothes and furniture stores. Its entry into the High Street was by a narrow pend under a dwelling house. Another route into the High Street from Wooer Street was Tolbooth Street, sometimes jocularly called "the shortest street in Scotland." Off Tolbooth Street opened Fleshmarket Court, one of the principal shambles of the town. To the east of Wooer Street several closes led into Wooer's Court behind the Black Bull Inn.

No less disreputable was the Back Row, now called Manor Street. The term, Back Row, was used in medieval Scotland for the secondary road running parallel to the High Street along the bottom of gardens of High Street properties. The Back Row of Falkirk contained many second-hand shops selling clothes, watches, tools and a thousand and

Wooer Street

one other items. It had lodging houses frequented by tramps, beggars, strolling street-singers and musicians. Last century it was not a recommendation to come from the Back Row which may have led to its change of name in 1898. Nevertheless it seems unfortunate that a name which had survived from the Middle Ages should have disappeared from the street index. Street names, unlike ma.ision houses, may be preserved at little cost to a local authority.

The entry into Kirk Wynd from the High Street until early this century was no wider than would accommodate a cart. At the corner on the left stood the Railway Tavern. Beyond the junction with the Back Row the Kirk Wynd narrowed, a large building jutting out from the east side. Behind this building ran a short lane, Earl's Lane, bending from Manor Street into Kirk Wynd. In a large scale demolition all the area from Manor Street to Bank Street was cleared away to make room for the modern Co-operative Store and its neighbouring shops.

Kirk Wynd

Manse Place, leading to the Parish Church, is a very old lane. On its north side stood the Manse with its garden running down to Newmarket Street.

Bank Street takes its name from the Falkirk Union Bank which stood at the northeast corner of the street. In 1803 the bank was founded amid high hopes which were dashed in 1816, tragic scenes being enacted before its closed doors as investors vainly clamoured for repayment. In 1820, undeterred by any superstitious consideration, the Commercial Banking Company set up their sign above the door. After this company moved to the building opposite Cow Wynd in 1832, the old Bank building became a private residence and then a school for Young Ladies. Ultimately the Inland Revenue restored the financial bias of the premises in 1879 at a time when income tax stood at 3d. in the pound.

Another Bank Street building with a chequered career was the Congregational Church which opened its doors in 1802. A church connection continued after 1835 when the congregation dissolved, the Baptists for a time worshipping there. By 1846, however, it had become a coffee house and temperance hotel. In 1852 it was being used as a court house, with a new strong room built to house prisoners. It was this feature which may have attracted the Royal Bank to move into the premises. By 1856 with the Royal Bank ensconced in Burns Court, the Burgh Police Court had staked its claim, abandoning the building in 1860 when it became a private dwelling. In 1911 it renewed its public service when it housed the very first Labour Exchange of Falkirk. Today it still stands as part of Young's Stores on the south side of Bank Street.

The fortunes of the Evangelical Union Church and its transmutation to a picture house has been described in another chapter. To the west of the cinema stood Violet Grove, a property owned by Cooper Weir, the precentor at the West Church who is said to have named his house after a favourite hymn tune. The Salvation Army chapel adjoining, dates from 1910. At first the Army had to endure much opposition, opponents trying to disrupt their street marches, bands and singing. "It will all end in a short time" declared one die-hard objector. Falkirk is the better that this malicious prediction has proved unfounded.

Vicar Street

Round the corner of Bank Street in Kirk Wynd stood one of the five gates into Falkirk. Below Newmarket Street, Kirk Wynd became Vicar's Loan or Vicar Street. On its east side there was the entry to the Grand Theatre which had a successful existence from 1903 until 1929 when like so many other theatres, it suffered in competition with talking pictures. Today the Regal Cinema (ABC) now occupies the site. The Post Office at the corner of Weir Street, only newly abandoned in favour of the new Post Office on the opposite side of the street, was built on what was a pleasant dwelling house and garden. At the lower part of Vicar Street a narrow footbridge crossed the railway line forcing traffic to go by way of McFarlane's Crescent. The coming of the tramway in 1905 saw the present road bridge being constructed.

Grahamston Bridge

Newmarket Street at the end of the 18th century was a rough track leading across the Glebe of the Parish Church from Vicar's Loan to the West End. In 1785 the opinion was being expressed that it "would be advantageous if the back road leading from the Manse to the West End of the Town at John Brock's House were repaired and made commodious for carriages." John Brock's House occupied the site where later the Crown Inn was built and now accommodates the

116

Royal Bank. In answer to this proposal the Rev. John Aitchison agreed to sell part of the Glebe, the sum received being all of £5.

It was not, however, until 1815 that some widening was carried out, and indeed not until much nearer the end of the 19th century before the terracing of Upper and Lower Newmarket Street was completed.

Newmarket Street

Newmarket Street gets its name from the new grain market established there in 1830. The story of the Corn Exchange, Dr. Corbet's House and garden and the Town Hall is told elsewhere.

One point of difference between Newmarket Street earlier this century and the present thoroughfare was that until 1924 there was no through road to Princes Street, the east side of Kirk Wynd continuing unbroken into Vicar's Loan. The ceremony of opening the way for east-west traffic was performed by the Prince of Wales, later Edward VIII.

Another significant difference was that the Lint Riggs was a very narrow lane not more than a few feet across. The name "Lint" denotes a connection with linen cloth but there are no historical records to indicate if flax was once grown here or linen produced or sold. The entrance to the High Street was by an iron gate.

Old Lint Riggs

Yet another difference early this century was the narrowness of the West End. Partly to blame were the Directors of Aitken's Brewery who resisted the surrender of ground for road widening. Aitken's founded in the 1730s at first used water brought by cart from a local well. In 1830, however, artesian wells were sunk delivering water at the rate of 200 gallons a minute. There is a measure of sadness that Falkirk's oldest industrial concern should have recently closed its doors.

At either corner of Glebe Street stood important buildings erected in 1879. On the east side the Y.M.C.A. provided an assembly place for youth. Thanks to a gift of £1,000 from Mr Robert Dollar, it supplied Falkirk with one of its earliest libraries at the important time when education was being made compulsory.

The Burgh Buildings on the west side of Glebe Street gave local government a permanent centre. It is interesting to reflect that in these walls were made the decisions which went so far to shape modern Falkirk.

Newmarket Street to some of our older citizens will conjure up many memories—the cobbled street, the umbrella on the wall above Yuill and Leckie's, the Wellington Statue, the excitements of election nights, the tolling bell of St. Andrew's Kirk, the trams protestingly rounding the line from Vicar Street at the Salon Super Cinema, cattle driven on the hoof to the Cattle Mart opened in 1875, the Auction

Rooms grimly significant in the Depression Years, the old Fire Engines, bells jangling, exiting from their station beyond the Town House, the railings that once enclosed the trim gardens between Upper and Lower levels of the street, the old name "the Boulevard," revived in one of our modern restaurants.

West End

The area where Hope Street joins West Bridge Street was for long used by travelling circuses and strolling players for their shows. In 1811 there was a determined bid to obtain this site for the rebuilding of the Parish Church instead of facing the expense of converting the medieval building. In 1868, however, the Sheriff Court was erected at this point, thus at last giving Falkirk a permanent court instead of having to house it in whatever suitable rooms were available in the Red Lion Inn, Rankine's Folly or the County Building in Bank Street.

In Hope Street was constructed the Burgh Library, opened in 1901 after a generous donation by Andrew Carnegie. Close by it in 1909 a roller skating rink had a brief existence before being converted into the equally short-lived Hippodrome, a picture and variety theatre.

Perhaps, however, the most celebrated feature of Hope Street is Brockville Park, the home of Falkirk Football Club. Falkirk Football Club was formed in 1876 and its first game was against Bonnybridge Grasshoppers. At that time Brockville was a sloping pitch flanked by green hedges. In 1882 the club moved permanently to Brockville. Perhaps its most famous moments were in 1913 and 1957 when it won the Scottish Cup.

"Better to widen than to wizen"—so runs the old saying. It would appear that Falkirk was long in heeding this particular piece of advice for until comparatively recently at few points did the south side of the town extend for more than a hundred yards from the High Street.

In this tightly packed area dwelled at least half of Falkirk's population living in close proximity to one another, sharing the same closes and stairs and what other amenities existed, and accepting as inevitable the congestion of shops, taverns, hostelries, coffee houses, churches, schools, assembly rooms, workshops, slaughter houses, smithies and stables.

At the East End, opposite the new shopping centre Burnhead Lane raises its cobbled face over the hill and drops towards where the East Burn bends out of Callendar policies. Though the burn has long gone underground and few houses remain along the length of the lane, enough is left of yesterday to recapture something of the atmosphere of the early century. Gone, however, are the piggeries which used to lie to the south of this roadway. Here, and even more importantly at Woodlands, townsfolk had "runs" where they reared pigs, a most popular and lucrative pastime until the turn of this century. It was a common sight to see pig owners scavenging around the town on the quest for "brock," the name given locally to pig swill. Wags used to refer to these piggeries as Falkirk's "Soo-logical Gardens." Perhaps because of this prolific supply of pork, the price was sixpence a pound in 1890.

To the west of Burnhead Lane remains a fragment of what was once an important offshoot from the High Street, Dundee Court. The temptation to seek some connection between Falkirk and the famous East Coast port is removed when among the property owners of as long ago as 1647 is one, James Dundie, though who or what he was is not recorded.

The Cross Keys Inn is of course well-known as that hostelry in which Robert Burns spent a night on his visit to Falkirk in 1786. The Cross Keys was but one of numerous taverns and inns along the High Street. A scrutiny of an old 19th century map will reveal a large number of houses marked "P.H." indicating a room set aside for the sale of ale and spirits. Like many towns last century Falkirk had an unenviable record of drunkenness. The pages of old copies of the Falkirk Herald tell all too frequently of brawls, wife beatings and child neglect arising from drink. In a perverse way the citizens of Falkirk were inclined to take pride in their reputation of being the most drunken provincial town in Scotland. Indeed there is a remarkable correspondence in which Falkirk competed with Airdrie for this dubious honour, and with more than 800 convictions for

Cross Keys Inn

drunkenness, won the day. Perhaps it was, however, more a commendation of the efficiency of the burgh's police than a censure on the inordinate capacity or lack of self-control of the population.

Though the chief entry into Falkirk from the south over many centuries has borne a number of names, quite the most consistently used has been Cow Wynd. One common error, often repeated, is to give as the origin of this name the droves of cattle entering and leaving the town by this route at the time of the Trysts. Cow Wynd had, however, been so called for long before the first Tryst, and perhaps even from the earliest beginnings of the town.

From feudal times the common pasture lay to the south and west of what is now Booth Place. Access to these grazing grounds was by way of the Cow Wynd, hence the name. The earliest Cow Wynd seems to have run from the High Street only as far as the old gate which stood somewhere about the junction with Booth Place. Beyond this point the road was called the Common Loan or the Cow Loan. In 1655 we read, of "the Common Loan that passeth from the Kow Wynd of

121

Falkirk." Along this Loan, behind where the present-day weigh-bridge is located, lay the Common Washing Green, Drying Green and Bleachfield. In 1791 there was a request for "a foot road on the East side of the Cow Loan beginning where the Cow Wynd terminates and leading to the Washing Green." Much later the Burgh Stables and Electricity Works were constructed on the washing green.

There was good reason for wishing a foot road. Cow Wynd was notoriously rough and filthy. Obviously the daily traffic of cattle fouling the road and the churning up of the earthen track were partly to blame. After the mid-18th century with the development of the Carron Iron Company and other local industries, the state of the road became worse because coal from Shieldhill and Glen Village was drawn in heavily laden carts by teams of horses along Cow Wynd, the only road from the south until the opening of Cockburn Street in 1927. It was perhaps appropriate that for a brief period about 1776 the name Coalhill Road was used but it was hard to make the public abandon the familiar Cow Wynd.

Cow Wynd

122

With the opening of the High Station in 1842 horse drawn buses bringing passengers down to the town added to the existing traffic. Perhaps the most famous of these was the Tartan Bus which bore customers to the Royal Hotel. One further hazard to be encountered were the number of outside stairs which jutted into the road making an already too narrow route even more of a bottleneck. The width of the entrance of the Cow Wynd from the High Street was at one time only thirteen feet.

In 1888 the Town Council returned to the battle over the name. "Cow Wynd" was not in their opinion "a very pretty name" and the civic fathers revealed not only their conspicuous disregard for tradition but also surprising lack of good taste in preferring "High Station Road," a name which continued officially until 1906 when officialdom bowed to the inevitable and reverted to the time-honoured name which the public had disdained to forsake, "Cow Wynd."

A prominent feature of the Cow Wynd still is the strangely shaped Tattie Kirk. Further along the East side past where Kidd's smithy stood, the local Co-operative Society built a new store on the site of what was once the Bowling Green Tavern in St. Crispin's Place. Behind was one of Falkirk's oldest bowling clubs, and at the end of each season a tent was erected in front of this tavern and in more ways than one the members gave the old season a spirited burial.

The Drill Hall close by dates from '859. Falkirk Volunteers had drilled in a variety of places, the Claydens, the Old Glebe, the Corn Market. Now they had their own drill hall but were not averse to sharing it with choral and dramatic groups wishing to stage concerts.

Comely Park House gave its name to the area in which it stood though it was a name imported from Glasgow. Comely Park School or as it was jocularly called in its early days after its first headmaster, "Cochrane's Academy" opened in 1879.

Up to 1845 the responsibility for the poor of the area rested on the parish. In that year the burgh assumed this duty and where Mr James Booth, gardener, had had his nurseries, a Poor's House and an asylum for lunatic paupers was built. An old plan indicating the layout of women's and men's quarters, work areas, dormitories and refectories, emphasises the spartan lot of those unhappy enough to enter the grim doors which did not finally close until 1905. The discharge of sewage from the Poor's House into the Gote Burn which flowed into the West Burn was a cause of great concern in the late 19th century when Falkirk became sensitive to and conscious of public health. After 1905 the building was used as a Model Lodging House until the First World War when it became a training centre and finally it served as the County Trades School.

Beyond this point the road to the High Station was a pleasant rural walk. To the right where Rennie Street now stands were wide pastures while on the left wooded plantations stretched up over the Coalheughbrae to Glen Village.

Cow Wynd, High Station Road, Coalhill Road, Kow Wynd—each of its several names echoes back across the centuries its own distinctive sound, the snarl of modern traffic, the creaking, jolting, horse-drawn station bus, the rumbling coal carts, the lowing herd . . .

Falkirk Savings Bank had opened its first premises in 1845 and ultimately occupied the corner site at Cow Wynd. King's Court which adjoins gets its name from the King's Arms Tavern which used to stand in this close, a neighbour of one of the town's best regarded coffee houses and through time the site of the first Registrar's Office in Falkirk.

The Falkirk Herald Office deserves special mention. The first edition of what was to be the local newpaper for a wide area around Falkirk was produced on 14th August, 1845. It was at that time a monthly journal founded by Alexander, a brother of James Hedderwick, who founded and edited the Glasgow Citizen. At first the Falkirk Herald was printed in Glasgow. Almost a year later the paper was bought by Archibald Johnston, a local printer. It was he who issued on 13th August, 1846, the first copy of the Falkirk Herald published and printed in Falkirk. From that time the proprietorship of the newspaper has remained within the Johnston family. In 1850 the paper was published as a weekly with Thursday the day of issue. At various times attempts were made to increase the frequency of publication but a Tuesday edition was soon abandoned. Wednesday for a time was the main publication day.

In 1883 Fred Johnston became proprietor and the Herald was transformed into a modern unit. The telephone was introduced in 1889 and soon new type-setting and rotary presses revolutionised production. Branch offices were established at Linlithgow, Bo'ness, Denny and Grangemouth. The old Herald Office was demolished in 1908 and the present building erected on the same site. Since that date the Falkirk Herald has kept abreast of technical developments in the newspaper world and has established itself firmly as the local newspaper.

A little to the west of the Herald Office stands one of Falkirk's most historic buildings. Where Watson's shoe shop is now located once stood the Great Lodging, the town house of the Livingstones of Westquarter. In due course it became the property of Dr Graham whose widow played hostess to Prince Charles on the night of the Battle of Falkirk. Behind the Great Lodging ran what was called Westquarter Wynd, nowadays Baxter's Wynd. The word Baxter is of course the old Scots term for a baker and no doubt it is from some baker's oven that the wynd is named. For a brief period in 1840 it was called Post Office Close but soon reverted to its previous name. Early last century it boasted two slaughter houses, one bakery and a candle maker's workshop. The Town Council of 1831 directed a special broadside against the fleshers of Baxter's Wynd who let blood and offal run into the sewers of the lane. A notable building in Baxter's Wynd was the Wheatsheaf Inn with its distinctive inn sign. This was a tavern much used by Sunday churchgoers who spent the time between morning and afternoon services therein. The local wags used to say that the singing in the afternoon was always louder and heartier than at the morning service.

The Cistern at Cistern Lane

A street no longer to be seen once ran between Baxter's Wynd and Robert's Wynd. This was Cistern Lane so called because it was here that a cistern was erected in 1805 to supply the town with water. It was built in what had been the garden of the Great Lodging. A plaque on its wall read as follows:

"This house is built to contain the water cistern or reservoir to serve the inhabitants of Falkirk under the direction of the Stentmasters." Its dimensions were 18 feet long, 11 feet wide and 9 feet deep and it held 13,330 gallons. Leaden pipes carried the water to the town wells. The original cistern had to be replaced in 1825. Ultimately the building was pensioned off and ended its career as a public convenience.

In Cistern Lane also stood an Auld Lichts Chapel which in the course of its time served several congregations—Auld Lichts, Wesleyans, Quakers and Highland drovers come to the Tryst for whom services in Gaelic were organised. In 1863 the last phase of its career was as a Music Hall.

Robert's Wynd, once called Bantaskine Wynd, passed under one of the old ports leading out of Falkirk into the Pleasance. The term "Pleasance" is used in Scotland to denote gardens on the outskirts of a town. Quite the most renowned building in the Pleasance was Rankine's Folly built in 1802 as Assembly Rooms. The Folly was repaired in 1852 and became the chief meeting place for many organisations and all manner of activities from church services to cock fighting, from variety entertainments to school examinations, from dances at feeing days to the headquarters of the Falkirk Town Mission. Today the Public Baths occupy the site.

Rankine's Folly

Sword's Wynd

Off Robert's Wynd ran the Howgate which for long was notorious for its dirt and squalor and for being one of the most unhealthy parts of the town. From the Howgate, roughly from where the backdoor of Woolworth's now stands, one of Falkirk's most important wynds used to climb. At one time it was called the Burnegait but after the Sword family made their residence there in the 17th century it became known as Bailie Sword's Close and later simply Sword's Wynd. The Bailie was the Procurator-Fiscal for the Burgh of Regality. Several inns and halls were built along this wynd. Baptists, Church of Christ and members of the Evangelical Union had their meeting places in Sword's Wynd. Here, too, before new premises were acquired in Bank Street and later Hope Street, the Sheriff Court met in the Corn Exchange Inn. There was also a Temperance Hotel and a Reading Room. All that is left of the wynd today is that cul-de-sac leading past Boots to the side door of Woolworth's store which has been built over the long curving flight of steps which led down to the Howgate.

Still further west along the High Street, roughly where Marks and Spencer have their store stood Burns Court named after the Burns family who for a time were owners of Gartcows Estate and were well-known lawyers in the 18th century. It was in Burns Court that Young Glengarry was carried to die after the sad accident which almost caused a clan feud on the day following the Battle of Falkirk. A Jewish synagogue stood in Burns Court.

The only other wynd of note towards the west end of the High Street ran between Sutherland's the Fishmongers and the Old Post Office. This was Bell's Wynd which dropped down to the junction of the Howgate and Cockburn Street and was much used by residents of Gartcows and Woodlands before Cockburn Street was opened up in 1927.

High Street, West

In the last 80 years development has gone on in the region south of this older part of the town. Notable citizens of their day have their names perpetuated in street names—James Booth, nursery owner, Provost Griffiths, William Hodge, sometime owner of Burnhead, later known as Woodlands, John Heugh, at one time owner of Gartcows, A. C. Rennie, actuary with the Falkirk Savings Bank, member of the School Board and Town Councillor, W. W. Neilson senior technical adviser to the Burgh of Falkirk last century, Bailie Robert Learmonth.

Today the southern boundary of Falkirk extends far beyond those streets and numerous citizens have their homes over a mile from the town centre, underlining the great changes which have come since the day when the Gote Burn, flowing along Hodge Street, marked the limit of the burgh's jurisdiction.

A century or so ago at a time when walking was more highly rated as a pastime than it is now, the stroll "up the back o' Jenny Mair's" was most popular with families and courting couples. To make the same journey today affords more interest to the antiquarian than to the lover of scenic charm for, while every few yards bring a peculiar echo of auld lang syne, little remains above ground and the green pastures and wide spaces through which the West Burn once wound are now built over.

To halt at the lowest dip in Camelon Road opposite the Municipal Buildings is to stand where once the Westburn Bridge spanned the Burn. Looking to the north from this point it was once possible to see the burn bend busily through a line of tannery pans before dropping out of sight towards Kilns House and that culvert which carried it under the railway and the Forth-Clyde Canal on its way to meet the Carron at the west side of Carron Bridge. In the fields which once lay to the north of Westburn Bridge General Hawley encamped his army on that fateful 17th January, 1746.

A few yards on the Camelon side of the bridge an old milestone by the roadside bore the legend "Stirling 11 miles, Edinburgh 24 miles, Linlithgow 8 miles." as if to remind its readers that it marked a stage on one of Scotland's oldest routes.

To the east the ground rises steeply up the Tanner's Brae. Wellside Place cuts off to the left towards the Kiln's Well to which it owes its name, while back in West Bridge Street where now Laurie's Garage stands, a line of small cottages marched uphill, their quaint outside stairs guarded by iron railings on which children were wont to swing and whose steps unashamedly professed their age by their deep worn treads.

The most conspicuous feature on the brae was the Gentleman Fountain. It was erected in 1871 on the approximate site of the old West Port by Patrick Gentleman with money provided by his brother, Bailie John Gentleman, who had a draper's business immediately to the west of Robert's Wynd. On the day when this typically Victorian monument was ceremonially dedicated, the Provost drank the health of Bailie Gentleman and prayed that the water would long flow and that nothing would be done "to injure such a beautiful

Houses at Tanners' Brae

structure." Alas, he did not count on the tyranny of the motor car whose brash insistence in 1923 dictated that the fountain be removed so that the corner could be widened.

In 1927, anticipating the needs of the new Infirmary which was soon to replace the old hospital at Victoria Park, Cockburn Street was at last breached to provide a vehicular route southwards from the west end of the High Street. Until that date an unbroken line of shops and houses stretched from the High Street down to Chapel Lane at the side of the West Church. Named after Provost Malcolm Cockburn the new road brought relief to the congestion in Cow Wynd.

Leaving the West Bridge behind and turning into Burnfoot Lane, we pass over the site of Dick's Tannery with its sour smelling tan pits fed by water from the burn. Tanning was a sizeable industry and locally made saddles, shoes and hats were deserving of the high reputation they enjoyed. The West Burn was not, however, always a friend. On several occasions there are records of the tan pits being damaged by excessive flooding.

Further along the Lane stood the Aerated Water Works of Barr established in 1830 and now with a modern trading empire in Glasgow, Wishaw, Irvine, Greenock and Kirkcaldy. Opposite the foot of Bell's Wynd and at the end of Burnfoot Lane, Jenny Mairs Burn turned sharply southwards along the line of modern Cockburn Street.

Last century a wooden bridge was constructed at Bell's Wynd while a a line of stepping stones provided a crossing from the Howgate.

Walking beside the open stream between Arnothill and the Pleasance one would have passed through the remains of the Antonine Wall. In this area too there was built in 1879 the Falkirk Academy. In this present age which at least pays lip service to the ideals of equal opportunity in education, there is something lamentable in its prospectus which claimed to cater "for children of a better class." Obviously snobbery like patriotism is not enough. The Academy closed in 1885 and was taken over by the Falkirk Burgh School Board as Arnothill School. When the new High School in Rennie Street opened in 1897 the school buildings were converted into Police Houses.

Arnothill is on record in the 18th century as Arnot's Hill which suggests a property owner. However a poem of last century mentions "arnuts" or earthnuts being collected there.

At the corner of what is now Hodge Street the West Burn received the waters of Adam's Gote. This burn rose in the high ground above Parkfoot and flowed down the east side of Cow Wynd as far as Comely Park School beyond which it passed under the road emerging in Hodge Street. On the way it collected its own tributary a stream which rose at Bower's Well in Gartcows Road close to the present-day Falkirk Laundry and fell rapidly down the hillside between what are the gardens of Neilson Street and Woodlands Crescent, joining the Gote beside the Erskine Church.

Opposite the Church the West Burn swung westward along what is now Garthill Lane between the Infirmary and Arnothill. Here it was fed by yet another burn coming down off Major's Loan. Further on still the West Burn may be traced beyond Maggie Wood's Loan where it enters a culvert. Its source is, however, debatable.

Maggie Wood's Loan is said to have been given its name because of the magpies which nested there. There is, however, a Maggie Wood who was a tenant of Easter Bantaskine in 1718. Bantaskine is recorded for many centuries. The laird of Pantasken figures prominently in 17th century history. The origin of the name is doubtful though there have been suggestions that it is derived from Gaelic "Pet-an-t'soisgel" a gospel croft.

It was at the corner of Cockburn Street where the West Burn turned out of Garthill Lane that Jenny Mair's cottage may have stood. She was probably the daughter of Michael Muir or Mair and Janet Livingstone in which case she was born in 1780. Her father was a well-known joiner. There is a 19th century jingle which starts, "Michael Mair made a chair." It is on record that Jennie sat at her spinning wheel by the door of her humble home and was "the picture of cleanliness in her old-fashioned mutch." Her sole claim to fame and immortality is that her house was a convenient walking distance from the town along a popular route and at a prominent bend in the stream so that through time woman and burn became identified with each other.

In 1871 a fateful decision was reached which has gone far to consign Jenny and her burn to oblivion. Complaints had been voiced of the serious flooding that followed heavy rain. Foul smells in dry weather produced as many complaints as impassable roads in wet. In 1871 the waters of the West Burn were piped and over 2,000 cartloads of earth filled in its bed. It did not go underground, however, without a struggle. The bore of pipes used was too small so that after a heavy fall of rain a miniature lake four feet deep was created and residents in Woodlands and Arnothill had to use waggons in order to pass dryshod about their business. After long agitation wider culverts were provided in 1901.

So passed out of sight one of Falkirk's most prominent features which long marked the western limits of the town, a burn where countless generations of young folk have paddled and fished for minnows, a burn along whose banks a legion of common folk have found a simple pleasure in strolling "up the back o' Jenny Mair's."

CHAPTER XII

THE END OF AN AULD SANG

No period in the long story of mankind has witnessed as marked an improvement in living standards as has the hundred years which have just passed. An analysis of this striking advance would undoubtedly underline the scientific and medical revolution, education for all, the extension of the franchise, the success of Trade Unions in obtaining a more equitable distribution of the profits of industry between Labour and Capital, benevolent attitudes of successive national governments towards social welfare.

However to omit the very real contribution of local government to the creation of a healthy society liberally supplied with the amenities which go to enhance the good life is to deny credit to a most deserving agent of reform. It is only just and fitting to pay tribute to the men and women who, without concern for financial reward, have voluntarily laboured to shape a new society. The fact that effective local government in Falkirk dates only from the last years of the Victorian era makes their achievement in this burgh the more remarkable. Their memorial is what Falkirk has become, their reward, the realisation that they have contributed in the relatively short span of four generations to a prodigious revolution in the way of life.

The extent of this transformation may be gauged by contrasting the community of a century ago with that of today. In the last quarter of the 19th century new housing erected between Hodge Street and Gartcows Road, between Meeks Road and James Street and in the Orchard Street area did little to keep pace with rising population which trebled itself between 1860 and 1900. That feature of Victorian times, the large family, resulted in severe overcrowding, families of ten and upwards occupying single and two-roomed houses. By the turn of the century Falkirk's 29,000 people were clamouring for more living space.

Many homes still relied on water from old wells and pumps. Some householders indeed even after the new supply gushed from their taps preferred "the taste of the old water" and continued to use former sources to the exasperation of health authorities. Sanitary provision was far from adequate, outside dry privies being not

133

Falkirk in the late 19th century

unusual, and, where they existed, water closets being shared by a number of families. Periodic visitations of killer infections—smallpox, diptheria, scarlet fever, typhus, enteric disorders, tuberculosis—seemed, even to a less germ-conscious age, to be not unconnected with congested houses and bad drains. Strangely, the most feared of all diseases, the largest single cause of mortality listed in burgh statistics, was measles, whose change of character over the century must surely be of social as well as medical interest. At a time of low wages and great unemployment with no welfare schemes outwith charity and the Friendly Societies, the diseases of malnutrition were rife. In 1901, at the time of recruitment for the Boer War, there was acute public concern at the numbers of young men rejected as unfit for military service. The introduction of school meals and medical inspection in schools in 1906 were not unrelated results. One other reason for disquiet lay in the fact that the old Infirmary opposite Victoria Park was already insufficient for the demands of an expanding community.

Proceedings in the Town Council in the 1890s point to other major problems. Where was the money to come from to expand the gas supply and to introduce "the electricity?" A public transport system was also an urgent need as housing spread and as many "indwellers" found employment "beyond walking distance of home."

134

Despite compulsory education there was much illiteracy. Frequent cases appeared in the burgh court of parents failing to provide education for their children. The problems met by the school boards when they were set up in 1872 had been far from resolved. Overcrowded classes and insufficient classrooms were unfortunately to be enduring perplexities. For a time the actual work of teaching was beset with unnecessary difficulties. Faced with the tyranny of the annual inspection in which each child was inspected separately, teachers could do nothing imaginative outwith the narrow confines of the approved syllabus. A bad report meant possible withdrawal of the government subsidy and a consequent extra burden on the rates. Thus the drilling of the less able to parrot the correct answers at the appropriate time was carried out at the expense of the academically better endowed. As a result a dead level of attainment was all that could be achieved. The better-off parents could of course secure more individual attention for their children in fee paying establishments, adding an educational inequality to the wide social gulf dividing the classes. The tragedy was that so many potentially bright children had to leave school when 12 years of age.

School Boards were careful with available funds and the minutes of their proceedings reveal disputes of comic proportions when set against modern educational practice. Should there be "new steel pens" or the "quills" of former years necessitating constant sharpening by the schoolmaster. Could they afford small chairs for small children instead of having "them sitting all days legs dangling?" Should gas lamps be installed or were oil burners sufficient? Were books other than "Testaments" required? Were Music and Art "fripperies"?

With long working hours and large families to rear, there was not time or money for leisure activities on the modern scale. Church organisations with their choirs, Dorcas Societies and discussion circles, were well attended. Soccer was beginning to attract players and spectators and an active local league was in being by the 1880s. At least two bowling clubs were in existence. Cock fighting, though illegal, is recorded as late as 1915. Wrestling and boxing contests drew a steady following. Cricket, cycling and pedestrianism were other minority pursuits. A large and enthusiastic audience could always be counted on for variety shows and concerts, and the social evening with or without dancing could be certain to pack the Town Hall, Rankine's Folly or the Drill Hall. Summer holidays were luxuries few could afford, and for the vast majority the highlights of the years were the Sunday School trip, perhaps a horse-drawn excursion to the hillfoots of the Ochils or to Linlithgow Loch, and the Tryst weekend. Unfortunately the chief leisure-time activity for too many was the public house and drunkenness brought before the local magistrates the inevitable pay day catalogue of brawls, assaults, wife beatings, swearing, breaches of the peace, and child neglect.

In 1890, then, when the abdication of the Feuars at last left the Town Council completely in charge of local affairs, there was much to daunt even the most ardent Town Councillors, ambitious to reshape their town. Yet in the following years, and especially after the Local Government Act of 1929, successive Councils have gone far to remedy the evils and deficiencies with which they were faced.

New Council Housing Schemes at Bainsford, Langlees, Windsor Road, East Carmuirs, Bog Road, Merchiston, Camelon and Callendar Park and private developments at Slamannan Road, Gartcows, Woodlands, Maggie Wood's Loan and Garden Street areas have not only heightened living standards but have dramatically changed the geography of the town. The long congested High Street has virtually become deserted as a residential district, and there are those who question if it has been in the best interests of the community to push population to the outskirts. One of the major problems of present-day local government is to devise means of bringing life back to the burgh centre after shops and offices are closed for the day. Nevertheless the Town Council has done a remarkably fine job in planning the extension of the town without unduly disrupting civic life, and ensuring that the public well-being has been given precedence over private gain of the landlord and speculative builder. Falkirk, like Rome, was not built in a day. New housing after 1919 was of modest proportions, but since the Second World War Falkirk may be proud of its achievement which places it very high in the list of Scottish Burghs most successful in the quality and quantity of housing.

The population, increasing to 33,000 in 1920 to its present 37,574, together with the astonishing growth in demand for water for domestic and industrial uses, forced a massive rethinking of the problem. In 1935 the first sod was cut in the project which created Loch Carron behind its dam, thus ensuring the town of an abundant and safe water supply. The burgh also built an efficient sewage disposal plant at Dalderse and an up-to-date cleansing plant. Epidemics continued to take their toll. Spanish influenza after the First World War claimed its victims as did Asian 'flu in the 1960s. Smallpox produced a major scare in 1920. However the advance of preventive medicine and the remarkable progress of medical science has brought significant reductions in the death rate, most notably in the area of infant mortality. The provision of a new Infirmary in 1932, now one of the foremost hospitals in Scotland, and more recently the establishment of clinics and teams of health visitors have substantially raised the standard of health in the community.

136

Until the time of nationalisation of gas and electricity, the burgh did well to arrange for supplies. Gas-lit streets and homes were common in the first three decades of the century and the errand for a new gas mantle is a childhood memory for many of the not so young. The excitement of first switching on electric light came to some Falkirk citizens as early as 1901 when the first generating plant was pressed into service, and to others after the extension of the works in 1919. It was not, however, until the 1930s that the majority of homes could have the benefit of this new and versatile source of power, and indeed gas lighting was not uncommon in Falkirk in the 1960s.

On 21st October, 1905 the first jolting, clattering unit of the "Silent Service" clanked its way along the High Street ushering in the tramway age with its distinctive sounds and excitements. Branches to Laurieston and a complete "circular" via Stenhousemuir and Larbert were soon added. To climb the circular stair to the open upper deck

Tram in High Street

of a Falkirk tram and journey with it along its swaying passage was a never-to-be-forgotten experience. On 21st July, 1936, amid scenes of not a little sentimentality and nostalgia, the last tram suitably bedecked made its obsequial procession to the depôt. A distinctive age had come to an end. In common with most tramways throughout the country, it had been forced to bow to the insistent competition of the more manoeuvrable motor bus. For some years before 1936 Falkirk had been witness to the hair-raising rivalry between Alexander's and Pender's Bus Companies. With Alexander's the victor, the pattern of public transport was set for the rest of the century.

Education has made impressive strides particularly after 1929 when the County Education Committee in which Falkirk was suitably represented took control. School building throughout the town has been noteworthy. Nursery and Primary Schools have been built in new housing areas. Special education of a high quality has been provided at Dawson Park. Secondary schooling has developed to meet the needs of a rising population and successive rises in the statutory school leaving age. Falkirk High School, the direct descendant of the Parish School and Grammar School which had served the community since the 17th century took up its new abode in Rennie Street in 1895, moving to its present Blinkbonny site only in 1962. In 1932 Falkirk Technical School provided the town with its second Senior Secondary School. In 1957 to avoid confusion with Falkirk Technical College, the school was renamed Graeme High School, and shortly afterwards in 1966 when the town and surrounding district were zoned, the school became the senior school for all children in the eastern part of the town. In this zoning arrangement Falkirk High School became the comprehensive senior secondary school for the western side of the catchment area. St. Mungo's High School, for long a four year secondary school, was reconstituted as the senior high school for all catholic children in Eastern Stirlingshire. Camelon High School became a junior high school linked with Falkirk High, and Woodlands High School in the old High School building in Rennie Street a junior high school linked with Graeme High School. One other significant change in the 1960s was the abandonment of the qualifying and control examinations, the so-called Eleven Plus, a formidable hurdle which roused great apprehensions in pupils and parents, seemed to brand children "success" or "failure" before they had even set foot within the secondary school, and erected social as well as educational barriers.

Higher education was not neglected. Though Falkirk failed in its bid to secure the "Fifth University," Stirling being preferred, it has had compensation in a fine Technical College and in the Teachers' Training College at Callendar Park.

Of consequence in the expansion of literacy was the provision of a well-stocked library in Hope Street for which the town was initially indebted to Andrew Carnegie. Not unimportant in the appearance and amenities of the town has been the provision of parks and open spaces for sport and relaxation.

During this century there has evolved in Falkirk a distinct community spirit. This may partly be explained by local newspapers awakening public conscience to common issues. Though the Falkirk Herald ultimately emerged as the principal local newspaper, it had for many years a formidable rival in the Falkirk Mail first published in 1886 at Grahamston Bridge. Its works moved in 1903 to Manor Street, and again in 1927 to Belmont Street where the last edition appeared in October, 1962. Because of the destruction of back numbers of the Falkirk Herald during the Second World War, it is to the Falkirk Mail that the local historian must turn for intimate details of the period before 1945.

Another cohesive element was the diversity in sporting, cultural and social activities, sufficient to attract many people from different backgrounds to participate one with the other, and thus in common achievement draw together with a sense of belonging to a closely knit community. It is not for nothing that Falkirk has become one of the key points in the Community Drama movement, her drama groups earning a nation wide reputation for the excellence of their performances. The annual "opera" staged by operatic societies has become a social as well as a theatrical landmark. Falkirk choirs, particularly the Caledonia Choir have earned countrywide renown. Women's Guilds, Burns Clubs, Masonic Lodges, charitable organisations, chess clubs, bridge clubs, homing pigeon groups, Women's Voluntary Service, church youth and adult activities, uniformed organisations, golf, bowling, curling, ice skating, cricket, tennis, football, rugby, swimming, cycling, athletics, and of course the ever popular football have brought interest and involvement to countless numbers of citizens. One organisation, Falkirk Archaeological and Natural History Society, has promoted an interest in the past and has contributed valuable papers on the history of the locality in its Proceedings. Another, Falkirk Arts and Civic Council, has had an important role in fostering all manner of cultural activities.

One certain reason for the development of a civic identity has been the sharing over the years of common experience as the events and movements of the twentieth century have unfolded—the first trams, the first Old Age Pensions, the first Labour Exchange, the widening of the Lint Riggs, the anguish of the First World War, the blacking out of windows, rationing, the great savings drive which reached a target of over £140,000, the welcome to returning soldiers, the War Memorial dedicated in 1926, the widening of Kirk Wynd and the West End, the opening of Princes Park, the gift of Dollar Park, the carillon of bells donated by Robert Dollar to the Parish Church, the Depression Years of the 1920s with foundries closing and on short time, the shock of the Redding Pit disaster, local strikes, the tension of the General

New Municipal Buildings

Strike with mass meetings of miners in Victoria Park, the opening of Cockburn Street and of Princes Street, the new Infirmary, talking pictures, the cruel years of want, unemployment and hardship of the 1930s, Alan Cobham and his flying machines, royal visits, keenly contested local and parliamentary elections, the Second World War, wartime cookery, salvage drives, A.R.P., the Home Guard, digging trenches and shelters, evacuees, the drive to buy a Spitfire, air raid warnings but fortunately no bombs, victory celebrations, vast new housing programmes, twinning with Quimper in 1950, the new Fire Station, the bi-centenary of Carron Iron Company, the last blast at Carron, the new town centre begun in 1962, the closing of the canals, the pleasure and sporting complex at Callendar Park and at the Stirling Road playing fields at Camelon, the new Municipal Buildings, Bobby McGregor winning his silver medal at the Tokyo Olympics, Falkirk twice winners of the Scottish cup, the designation of Falkirk-Grangemouth as a growth area.

The twentieth century, then, has witnessed a phenomenal change in the way of life in the Burgh of Falkirk. There is no place, however, for complacency. Serious social problems, some old, some new, are all too apparent. Sub-standard housing still exists. There is yet poverty in the midst of plenty. The motor car continues to present unresolved

140

difficulties in the congestion it brings to the town centre. And what immediate solution is there to problems such as alcoholism, violence, child neglect, battered babies, promiscuous sexual behaviour, vandalism, the care of the elderly, the use and abuse of leisure?

Falkirk has been a burgh restlessly confined within its boundaries, ever anxious to expand into adjoining districts. Though in 1900 Camelon was absorbed, other areas have been more coy. Larbert strenuously resisted determined approaches in 1911 and again in 1950. Grangemouth, too, has been most wary of a merger even though a most prosperous future awaits the full co-operation of the two burghs so happily located geographically and blessed with a huge reservoir of industrial skills. The advent of North Sea Oil has made their liaison even more assured. The shotgun in all these teetering marriages has been provided by the government in its Local Government Act of 1973 by which a large Central Region is to be created thus recognising the virtue of the larger administrative unit. There is of course disappointment in Falkirk that it has not been selected as the centre of the new region particularly when it is so much of its economic heart. Some consolation may be had from the thought that what is lost to the burgh will be found in the region.

As Falkirk prepares then to end its auld sang, I am confident that a thousand years of civic identity are not about to be buried. No matter how earnestly or subtly regional loyalties are fostered, it will be many years before the Bairns of Falkirk lose pride in their separate identity or lively interest in the accidents and designs, the individuals and multitudes, the single events and sweeping movements that since the Middle Ages have gone to fashion the history of Falkirk. The song may be ended, but in the words of the popular refrain, "the melody lingers on."

PROVOSTS OF THE BURGH

Henry Salmon	Nov. 1833 to Nov. 1836
James Aitken	Nov. 1836 to Nov. 1839
Thomas Aitken	Nov. 1839 to Nov. 1842
Robert Adam	Nov. 1842 to Nov. 1857
Robert Young	Nov. 1857 to July 1858
Thomas Kier	July. 1858 to Nov .1867
John Russel	Nov. 1867 to Nov. 1879
Malcolm Cockburn	Nov. 1879 to Nov. 1883
William Hodge	Nov. 1883 to Aug. 1889
Borthwick Watson	Sept. 1889 to Nov. 1892
Azariah Griffiths	Nov. 1892 to Nov. 1895
John Weir	Nov. 1895 to Nov. 1904
Archibald Christie	Nov. 1904 to Nov. 1910
James C. Bogle, O.B.E.	Nov. 1910 to Nov. 1919
James Gordon Russell	Nov. 1919 to Nov. 1922
William Muirhead	Nov. 1922 to Nov. 1925
John Cameron Gilchrist	Nov. 1925 to Nov. 1928
William Smith	Nov. 1928 to Nov. 1931
Archibald Grassam Logan	Nov. 1931 to Nov. 1934
William Stevenson	Nov. 1934 to Nov. 1937
Henry Begg	Nov. 1937 to Nov. 1943
James Strachan, O.B.E.	Nov. 1943 to Nov. 1946
Peter Symon	Nov. 1946 to May 1950
Andrew Wallace	May 1950 to May 1953
Robert Henry Watson	May 1953 to May 1956
James Paterson	May 1956 to May 1959
William B. Leishman, O.B.E.	May 1959 to May 1962
John Maxwell	May 1962 to May 1965
James Marshall	May 1965 to May 1968
William McCrae	May 1968 to May 1971
William Fenney	May 1971 to May 1974
James Mitchell	May 1974 to May 1975

SOURCES

FALKIRK PARISH REGISTERS.

REGISTRAR GENERAL'S REGISTERS OF BIRTHS, MARRIAGES AND DEATHS.

The STATISTICAL ACCOUNT of Scotland drawn up from the communications of the ministers of the different parishes by Sir John Sinclair. 1797 Volume 19.
(FIRST STATISTICAL ACCOUNT).

The NEW STATISTICAL ACCOUNT of Scotland, 1845.
Volume 8, Dumbarton, Stirling, Clackmannan.
(SECOND STATISTICAL ACCOUNT).

The THIRD STATISTICAL ACCOUNT of Scotland, the County of Stirling edited by R. C. Rennie. 1966. Collins.

The GRANGEMOUTH Falkirk regional survey and plan:
(prepared for) the Stirlingshire, West Lothian and Falkirk Growth Area Joint Planning Advisory Committee and Scottish Development Department (2 Volumes). Edinburgh: H.M.S.O. 1968.

PARLIAMENTARY PROCEEDINGS HOUSE OF LORDS, 1859 . . . Falkirk Police Bill.

BURGH OF FALKIRK: Records of the Town Council of Falkirk, 1833 to date.

BURGH OF FALKIRK: Stent Masters Records.

BURGH OF FALKIRK: Records of the Feuars of Falkirk.

THE FALKIRK HERALD: (and allied newspapers).

THE FALKIRK MAIL.

FALKIRK PARISH: Minutes of the Kirk Session (from 1617).

PRESBYTERY OF LINLITHGOW AND FALKIRK: Minutes.

MURRAY, George I. Records of Falkirk Parish: a review of Kirk Session Records of Falkirk from 1617 to 1888. (2 Volumes). Falkirk: Duncan and Murray 1887, 1888.

LAWSON, Lewis: The Church at Falkirk. Falkirk Old Parish Church. 1974.

LOVE, James: Local Antiquarian Notes and Queries (Reprinted from the Falkirk Herald). 4 Volumes. Falkirk: F. Johnston & Co. 1908-1928 (also unpublished material).

REPORTS OF THE MEDICAL OFFICER OF HEALTH: BURGH AND COUNTY ARCHIVES.

FALKIRK ARCHAEOLOGICAL AND NATURAL HISTORY SOCIETY: Proceedings.

RAILWAY ARCHIVE MATERIAL.

REPORT ON WORKING CONDITIONS OF YOUNG PEOPLE IN MINES. 1841-1843.

CAMPBELL, R. H. Carron Company. Oliver and Boyd. 1961.

EARLY HISTORY OF CARRON IRON COMPANY.

PRATT, Edwin A.: Scottish canals and waterways. Selwyn & Blount. 1922.

CADELL, H. M.: The industrial development of the Forth Valley IN The Scottish Geographical Magazine, February, 1904.

CADELL, H. M.: The story of the Forth. Maclehose. 1913.

VARIOUS histories of local firms: brief accounts issued in advertising material.

CALLENDAR ESTATE RECORDS.

HALDANE, A. R. B.: The Drove roads of Scotland. Nelson 1952.

144

THE ROYAL COMMISSION ON THE ANCIENT AND HISTORICAL MONUMENTS OF SCOTLAND. Stirlingshire: an inventory of the ancient monuments (2 Volumes). H.M.S.O. 1963.

FORBES OF CALLENDAR PAPERS.

FLEMING, J. S.:   Ancient castles and mansions of Stirling nobility.   Gardner. 1902.

HOLYROOD ABBEY CHRONICLE: Liber cartarum Sancte Crucis, edited by Cosmo Innes. Bannantyne Club. 1840.

MINUTES of Heritors.

THE ANTONINE WALL REPORT:
being an account of excavations, etc., made under the direction of the Glasgow Archaeological Society during 1890-1893.
Glasgow Archaeology Society. 1899.

ROBERTSON, Anne S.:
The Antonine Wall: a handbook to the Roman Wall between Forth and Clyde and a guide to its surviving remains.
Glasgow Archaeological Society. 1973.

MacDONALD, Sir George:
The Roman Wall in Scotland, 2nd ed. Clarendon Press. 1934.

CHRONICLES of Atholl and Tullibardine.

BLAIKIE Collection.

CHAMBERS, Robert:
History of the Rebellion in Scotland in 1745, 1746. 2 Volumes. Edinburgh, 1828.

TOMASSON, Katherine and BUIST, Francis:
Battles of the '45.
Batsford. 1962.

145

LAWSON, Lewis, editor:
>The Jacobites in Stirlingshire. Local History Panel of Stirlingshire Teachers of History. 1971.

DUKE OF CUMBERLAND'S ORDER BOOK.

THE BRITISH MAGAZINE, 1746.

THE SCOTS MAGAZINE, 1746.

THE CALEDONIAN MERCURY, 1746.

THE LONDON EVENING POST, 1746.

THE ALBEMARLE PAPERS.

ELCHO, Lord David:
>A short account of the affairs of Scotland in the years 1744, 1745, 1746, edited by E. Charteris. David Douglas. 1907.

REPORT of Proceedings of Board of General Officers on the examination of Sir John Cope.

HOME, John:
>The history of the Rebellion in Scotland in 1745. Peter Brown. 1822.

JOHNSTONE, James De Chevalier:
>Memoirs of the Rebellion in 1745 and 1746. Longmans. 1820.

LOCKHART PAPERS:
>Journals and memoirs of the Young Pretender's expedition in 1745.

NIMMO, William:
>A general history of Stirlingshire, 3rd ed. (2 Volumes). Hamilton, Adams & Co. 1880.

TAYLER, A. **and** H.
>1745 and after Nelson. 1938. (O'Sullivan's Narrative).

MEMORIALS of John Murray of Broughton, sometime Secretary to Prince Charles Edward, 1740/1747.
Scottish History Society. 1898.

MAXWELL, James of Kirkconnell:
Narrative of Charles Prince of Wales' expedition to Scotland in the year 1745.
Maitland Club. 1841.

ST. JAMES'S EVENING POST, 20th January, 1745-46.

CULLODEN PAPERS: (including reports by William Corse).

LORD GEORGE MURRAY'S JOURNAL:
Jacobite memories of the Rebellion in 1745.

BROWNE, James: History of the Highlands and the Highland Clans.
A. Fullerton & Co. 1838.

MARQUIS D'EQUILLES:
Account of Battle of Falkirk reprinted in Scotsman, 17th April, 1900.

HAWLEY'S ORDER OF 12th January, 1746, quoted in Home.

SETON, Bruce Gordon and ARNOT, Jean Gordon:
The Prisoners of the '45, 3 Volumes.
Scottish History Society. 1928-1929.

MAPS of streams and underground waters held by Burgh Engineer, Falkirk.

MAP of FALKIRK, 1833: drawn by Parliamentary Commissions.

MAPS dating from 1868 held by Falkirk Public Library

TRANSPARENCIES of Old Falkirk held by Falkirk Public Library (donated by Falkirk Archaeological Society).

PIERRE de LANGTOFT'S Chronicle.

WILLIAM OF MAMESBURY'S Chronicle: Falkirk Roll of Arms.

WALTER OF GUISBOROUGH'S Chronicle.

RISHANGER Chronicle.

FORDUN'S Chronicle.

SYMEON OF DURHAM: Monachi Opera Omnia.

SCOTT, Hew: Fasti Ecclesiae Scoticanae: the succession of ministers in the Church of Scotland from the Reformation.
Oliver and Boyd. 1915.

GEOGRAPHICAL COLLECTIONS relating to Scotland made by Walter Macfarlane, edited by Sir Arthur Mitchell.
Scottish History Society. 1906.

EXCHEQUER ROLLS:
Edward I.

HENRY THE MINSTREL:
The Actis and Deidis of the illustere and vailzeand Camioun Schir William Wallace Knicht of Ellerslie.

HEARN'S Chronicle.

HEMMINGFORD'S Chronicle.

INDEX